TRANSLATIONS OF FRENCH FICTION

To Mike and Teddo

TRANSLATIONS OF FRENCH SENTIMENTAL PROSE FICTION IN LATE EIGHTEENTH-CENTURY ENGLAND: THE HISTORY OF A LITERARY VOGUE · JOSEPHINE GRIEDER

DUKE UNIVERSITY PRESS DURHAM, N.C. 1975

© 1975, Duke University Press
L.C.C. card no. 74–81963
I.S.B.N. 0–8223–0327–2
Printed in the United States of
America by Heritage Printers

TABLE OF CONTENTS

INTRODUCTION

Literary taste is an ephemeral commodity. How to anticipate it, how to capitalize on it once it declares itself, how to accommodate it as it develops, how to exit gracefully before it shifts object: these are dilemmas that perpetually confront the commercially-minded author and publisher. If the past may serve as a reference for the future, then the vogue of a certain type of literature is well worth examination; for someone, somehow, found some means of capturing the public's interest for that period of time.

At the same time, literary taste reflects more than clever commercial manipulation. It illuminates the very public to which it belongs: the readers' concerns, the conventions which they are willing to accept, and the deviations they are willing to tolerate. Particularly when the literature in question is fiction rather than nonfiction, sifting through the statistics of a literary vogue can reveal an uncommon glimpse of the society which took delight in such productions.

Translations of French sentimental prose fiction were just such a vogue in late eighteenth-century England. Their popularity is a particularly good example of literary taste for two reasons. First, the literature was not indigenous to England. That is, while British writers of the period were producing sentimental novels and might naturally expect to win recognition on their home ground, the translations depended for their popularity on a deliberate campaign to introduce their foreign authors to the English public and to publicize the quality—and the novelty—of the fiction becoming available. Superimposing a foreign literature on an already thriving indigenous genre and gaining the public's acceptance of it argue a shrewd knowledge of the literary marketplace; but the enthusiasm with which the public greeted the translations and continued to demand them during several decades indicates as well that something in this translated foreign fiction satisfied particular expectations or needs of the British public.

Second, the duration of the popularity of translations from the French can be specifically defined, and its pattern of introduction, growing acceptance, enthusiastic demand, and decline can be demonstrated. From 1760 to 1764, translations began to infiltrate the British market, both in hardcover and in periodical form; the year 1765 marked the first definite interest in French sentimental fiction. For the two following decades translations gradually increased in number, until during the eighties and early nineties interest was at its height. Thereafter, although hardcover translations held their own, French fiction in the magazines all but disappeared from the scene. The beginning and the end, both identifiable, indicate that in fact translations of French sentimental fiction were not just a manifestation of international literary interest but a vogue peculiar to late eighteenth-century England.

That these translations formed a not inconsiderable part of the literature available to the English reading public is well known, thanks to the works of scholars like Ernest A. Baker, James R. Foster, Robert Mayo, J. M. S. Tompkins, and Walter Francis Wright.[1] Until now, this translated fiction has been considered with regard to its possible influence on English authors and the English literature of the period. This study is an attempt to approach the problem from a different point of view: to describe the literary milieu in which this foreign fiction was produced, to indicate the conditions which made such translations feasible and attractive, and to present the reactions of the British critics and public towards it. The bibliography of French sentimental authors and their works in English translation establishes in detail the scope of fiction available and clarifies references and information given in the first three chapters; the concluding index of English titles facilitates access to the bibliography.

At this point, several caveats may be in order. Because the focus of this study is the body of French sentimental literature which appeared in translation—its general characteristics and its reputation with its foreign audience—little attempt has been made to analyze its literary merits (characterization, plot structure, style); these belong more properly to a history of literary development and have many times been described by both English and French literary historians. Much mention is made of certain authors, whereas the contents of their works are seemingly ignored; but what is of consequence is, I feel, not the indi-

1. See Ernest A. Baker, *History of the English Novel.* Vol. V, *The Novel of Sentiment and the Gothic Romance* (London: Witherby, 1934); James R. Foster, *History of the Pre-Romantic Novel in English* (New York: Modern Language Association, 1949); Robert Mayo, *The English Novel in the Magazines, 1740–1815* (Evanston: Northwestern University Press, 1962); J. M. S. Tompkins, *The Popular Novel in England, 1770–1800* (1932; rpt Lincoln: University of Nebraska Press, 1961); Walter Francis Wright, *Sensibility in English Prose Fiction, 1760–1814: A Reinterpretation* (Urbana: University of Illinois, 1937); and, in testimony to American interest, Herbert R. Brown, *The Sentimental Novel in America, 1789–1860* (1940; rpt Chapel Hill: University of North Carolina Press, 1972).

viduality of any particular novel or story but the individuality of a French author or of fiction labelled "From the French" in the eyes of its contemporary readers and critics. Moreover, though it is tempting to speculate what the well-educated Englishman (or -woman) thought of these novels as he perused them in the original, the fact is that the vogue existed because of the mono-lingual British reader who was more than happy, as evidence will show, to accept the translations as a welcome addition to his literary fare.

This study, thus, is voluntarily circumscribed in intent. Perhaps it belongs as much to social or intellectual history as it does to the history of literature, for it is a commentary on the public which welcomed the translated fiction and on those who sponsored and encouraged its publication. As a study in comparative literature, it indicates at least that there are certain moments when the literary taste of two different nationalities coincides to a considerable degree.

TRANSLATIONS OF FRENCH FICTION

CHAPTER ONE. THE SOURCE OF
THE TRANSLATIONS

What was this French sentimental fiction that the English public read with such avidity? What conditions in France encouraged it? Who were the authors associated with it? A few generalizations will provide a perspective for the detailed study of its vogue in England.

The novels and tales published in France from 1760 to the 1790's can largely be categorized as sentimental fiction.[1] A precise definition of "sentimental" has always been elusive.[2] Roughly, it may be said that as its primary philosophical assumption, sentimentality held that the heart should take precedence over the head—in other words, that innate, spontaneous emotional impulse was a better guide to proper action than rational, detached analysis, although reason should subsequently be consulted. Following one's own inclinations—or, to use the contemporary and more accurate term, one's *sensibilité*—would necessarily produce the

1. Studies of French sentimental fiction are numerous; among the most comprehensive are André Monglond, *Le Préromantisme français*. Vol. II, *Le Maître des âmes sensibles* (Grenoble: Arthaud, 1930); Daniel Mornet, *Le Romantisme en France au XVIII*e *siècle* (Paris: Hachette, 1912); Henri Coulet, *Le Roman jusqu'à la Révolution* (Paris: A. Colin, 1967); Servais Etienne, *Le Genre romanesque en France depuis l'apparition de la "Nouvelle Héloïse" jusqu'aux approches de la Révolution* (Paris: A. Colin, 1922); Pierre Trahard, *Les Maîtres de la sensibilité française*. 4 vols. (Paris: Boivin et cie, 1931–33); and F. C. Green, *French Novelists, Manners and Ideas from the Renaissance to the Revolution* (New York: Appleton, 1929).

2. Those scholars cited in note 1 of the introduction and above comment in detail on the problem, as do I. H. Smith in "The Concept 'Sensibilité' and the Enlightenment," *AUMLA*, XXVII (May 1967), 5–17; Edith Birkhead in "Sentiment and Sensibility in the Eighteenth-Century Novel," *Essays and Studies*, II (1925), 92–116; and Eric Erämetsä in *A Study of the Word "Sentimental" and of Other Linguistic Characteristics of Eighteenth-Century Sentimentalism in England* (Helsinki, 1951). Further discussion of the subject may be found in works relating to the theater, such as Arthur Sherbo, *English Sentimental Drama* (East Lansing: Michigan State University Press, 1957), and Ernest Birnbaum, *The Drama of Sensibility* (Boston: Ginn, 1915).

most desirable moral behavior: sincere piety; filial and parental affection; virtue and fidelity; recognition of the individual, no matter what his rank; benevolence extended to the less fortunate.[3] One or more of these elements are enough to qualify as sentimental very diverse sorts of fiction: stories of love and passion, oriental tales, historical romances, pastorals, and didactic novels.

Equally characteristic of sentimental fiction was its avowed purpose to educate the reader morally. "Le plus digne objet de la littérature," began Marmontel's *Essai sur les romans*, "le seul même qui l'enoblisse et qui l'honore, c'est son utilité morale."[4] That this genre had by its very nature a considerable advantage over more rational forms of literary expression was often emphasized; for, since sentimental novels were concerned with *sensibilité* and its manifestations, they appealed to the reader's own emotions as well as to his intelligence and stimulated his moral awareness of others' sentiments and situations.[5] The most detailed apologist for this point of view, Romance de Mesmon, expressed

3. Here is a contemporary definition of *sensibilité* and its effects: "La Sensibilité est le principe qui met toutes les passions en mouvement; mais qui, en les opposant les unes aux autres, en adoucit toujours les effets; et de ce choc à peu près égal, de cet équilibre entre tant de sentimens divers, naît la vertu. Que la Raison l'éclaire et la dirige, le grand homme est formé. . . . Ami de l'humanité, parce qu'il sent qu'il est homme, il cherche à mettre plus d'égalité dans le bonheur de ses semblables; à déraciner des abus multipliés, et qui, tous introduits en faveur du puissant, ne tendoient qu'à opprimer le foible. Il adoucit la rigueur des loix, proportionne les châtimens aux délits, voit que les crimes des petits ne naissent, le plus souvent, que de l'oppression et du malheur, et qu'en les rendant heureux, on les rendra aussi moins criminels: c'est ainsi qu'il remonte aux premières causes des calamités publiques, pour en détruire plus sûrement les effets": Mistelet, *De la sensibilité, par rapport aux drames, aux romans, et à l'éducation* (Amsterdam et Paris, 1777), pp. 7–9. For further discussion of the aspects of *sensibilité* as manifested in literature, see below, chapter 3.

4. Jean-François Marmontel, *Essai sur les romans, considerés du côté moral*, first written in 1777 and collected in *Oeuvres complètes* (Paris: Verdière, 1819), X, 287.

5. Philippe van Tieghem emphasizes this new aspect of eighteenth-century criticism in *Petite Histoire des grandes doctrines littéraires en France*, 3rd ed. (Paris: Presses universitaires de France, 1950): "Sans cet enthousiasme pour la vertu, point de leçon de vertu efficace. On ne conçoit pas la leçon morale sans l'attendrissement" (p. 117).

it thus in his "De la lecture des romans: Fragment d'un manuscrit sur la sensibilité": "L'habitude de s'attendrir sur les malheurs imaginaires prépare le coeur à une véritable sensibilité; l'habitude de s'identifier avec l'homme de bien en action, nous accoutume enfin à trouver qu'alors nous remplissons notre place; nous nous mettons nous-mêmes sur la scene, et nous nous pénétrons de la situation de nos Héros."[6] And so by their presentation of diverse emotional situations, sentimental novels awakened the reader's moral sense and inspired him to emulate the worthy actions he read of. His moral betterment was thereby accomplished, as Mme de Staël envisioned it in her *Essai sur les fictions*: "Les fictions touchantes qui exercent l'ame à toutes les passions généreuses lui en donnent l'habitude, et lui font prendre à son insu un engagement avec elle-même, qu'elle aurait honte de rétracter, si une situation semblable lui devenait personnelle."[7]

This line of critical theorizing enhanced the novel's stature and dignity; for when teaching morality became the function of the novel, then fiction effectively displaced its two traditional rivals, philosophy and history. Moral philosophy might offer the reader truths, but coldly and repugnantly presented. The novel offered him —to use the expression which became a critical commonplace— "la morale mise en action"; and, as Mercier noted, a man who wouldn't read moral treatises "chérit le pinceau naïf et pur qui met

6. G.-H. de Romance de Mesmon, "De la lecture des romans: Fragment d'un manuscrit sur la sensibilité," *Journal de Lecture, ou Choix périodique de Littérature et de Morale*, VI (1776), 63. This essay was later printed in book form in 1785 and was prefaced by the glowing review from the *Journal des Savants* of 1778 which praised the author's "talent d'appercevoir et rendre sensible ce qui échappoit aux yeux ordinaires" (p. 6).

7. *Essai sur les fictions*, first written in 1795 and collected in *Oeuvres de Mme la Baronne de Staël-Holstein*, I (Paris: Lefèvre, 1838), 143. A number of other critics took up the cudgels on behalf of the novel's morality, among them Gilles Boucher de la Richarderie in his *Lettre sur les romans, adressée à Mme la Marquise des Ayvelles* (Genève, 1762), and even the Marquis de Sade, in "Idée sur les romans," which prefaced *Les Crimes de l'amour*, I (Paris, An VIII [1800]). For a full discussion of late eighteenth-century criticism, see my article "The Novel as a Genre: Formal French Literary Theory, 1760–1800," *French Review*, XLIV (December 1972), 278–290.

à profit la sensibilité du coeur humain, pour lui enseigner ce que l'intérêt personnel et farouche repousse ordinairement."[8] History, though instructive, suffered from two defects. First, it was often forced to deal with immorality but prohibited by objectivity from criticizing it; therefore, its lessons could not profit the reader. Second, it had no application to the common reader, speaking as it did "A un très-petit nombre d'hommes, aux princes, aux généraux, aux gouvernans." But the novel? "Un roman," continued the same critic, "est plus à la portée de nous autres gens vulgaires; il doit être aussi plus intéressant pour nous; ce sont nos coeurs, nos passions, c'est nous-mêmes que nous y retrouvons." And if the novel was more relevant to people of all classes, then its moral lessons were more effective. "La morale usuelle y est mise en action; on nous fait connaître nos maladies, on nous montre les remèdes; il ne tient qu'à nous de les prendre, et de nous les appliquer."[9]

The success of sentimental fiction, and the critical acclaim which accompanied it, had been slowly prepared during the first half of the century.[10] Most of the French novels before 1760 were intellectual, stylish, and witty—and, often, licentious enough to justify the critics' charges of immorality and inevitably pernicious effects. Nevertheless, germs of sentimental philosophy could be discerned in an occasional work: the involved analysis of the nuances of sentiment in Marivaux's *La Vie de Marianne* (1731–41); the confrontation between the innocent child of nature and worldly French society in Mme de Graffigny's *Lettres d'une Péruvienne* (1747); a noble's benevolence to a peasant couple in

8. Louis Sébastien Mercier, *De la littérature et des littérateurs* (Yverdon, 1778), p. 5

9. *Décade Philosophique*, no. 45 (30 messidor An III [1795]), pp. 161–162. The same argument appeared earlier in the *Année Littéraire*, I (1782), 29, less dramatically phrased.

10. Besides those general works already cited, Paul van Tieghem studies this specific period in "Le Roman sentimental en Europe de Richardson à Rousseau (1740–61)," *Revue de la Littérature comparée*, XX (1940), 129–151, and Geoffrey Atkinson considers it in *The Sentimental Revolution: French Writers of 1690–1740*, ed. A. C. Keller (Seattle: University of Washington Press, 1965).

Duclos' *Les Confessions du comte de **** (1742). The only consistent precursor of the sentimentalists, however, was the abbé Prévost; for his heroes and heroines in *Le Doyen de Killerine* (1735–40), *Les Mémoires et avantures d'un homme de qualité* (1728–31), and *Le Philosophe anglais, ou histoire de M. Cleveland* (1731–39) suffered from the conflict between *sensibilité* and social convention long before such friction became a standard plot device.

A significant impetus to the genre's establishment came from across the channel, with the translations of the novels of Samuel Richardson.[11] Thanks to the efforts of Prévost, *Pamela*, *Clarissa*, and *Sir Charles Grandison* all appeared in French before 1760. In spite of the abbé's considerable abridging, the novels' presentation of a variety of social classes, of natural and unforced sentiment, and of scrupulously moral behavior found great favor with the French public. "Tout ce que Montaigne, Charron, La Rochefoucauld et Nicole ont mis en maximes, Richardson l'a mis en action," proclaimed a typically enthusiastic reader, Denis Diderot, in his *Eloge de Richardson*.[12] "[En lisant ses romans] j'étais devenu spectateur d'une multitude d'incidents, je sentais que j'avais acquis de l'expérience. . . . Le monde où nous vivons est le lieu de la scène; le fond de son drame est vrai; ses personnages ont toute la réalité possible; ses caractères sont pris du milieu de la société; ses incidents sont dans les moeurs de toutes les nations policées; les passions qu'il peint sont telles que je les éprouve en moi; . . . les traverses et les afflictions de ses personnages sont de la nature de celles qui me menaient sans cesse; il me montre le cours général des choses qui m'environnent" (pp. 30–31). As works of other

11. See Harold Wade Streeter, *The Eighteenth-Century English Novel in French Translation: A Bibliographical Study* (New York, 1936); Joseph Texte, *Jean-Jacques Rousseau et les origines du cosmopolitanisme littéraire* (Paris: Hachette, 1895); and F. C. Green, *Literary Ideas in 18th-Century France and England, a Critical Survey* (New York: Ungar, 1966), for various aspects of this question.

12. *Eloge de Richardson* (originally published in the *Journal étranger*, janvier 1762), *Oeuvres esthétiques*, ed. P. Vernière (Paris: Classiques Garnier, 1965), p. 29, hereafter cited in the text.

English novelists became available in translation, French critics after 1760 continued to cite their portrayals of virtue in ordinary life as proof of the novel's utility—"des cours de morale pratique à l'usage de tous les états," as Bricaire de la Dixmérie said, in which "nul rang n'y est dédaigné."[13]

While literature was accustoming the reading public to fictional demonstrations of morality and sentiment, the French themselves were beginning to take more and more interest in their own emotional reactions; and particularly after 1770, *sensibilité* became the social catchword of the day.[14] Not kindly, Mme Riccoboni reported to her friend David Garrick in 1772, "Nous sommes actuellement dans une fureur de sensibilité, qui passe toute imagination; nos dames veulent pleurer, crier, étouffer aux spectacles. . . . Le sentiment est la folie du jour, on se l'est mis si fort en tête qu'il en reste bien peu dans le coeur."[15] Disapproving opinion was overwhelmed, however, by public enthusiasm for displays of sentiment. Benevolence, the most visible manifestation of *sensibilité*, motivated a multitude of charitable projects financed by both private and public means. Louis XVI and his queen contributed money to the poor in times of particular misery; hospitals and shelters for the indigent sprang up; multi-volume anthologies of anecdotes about benevolence poured forth.[16] Indeed, in 1783, Bacu-

13. Bricaire de la Dixmérie, "Discours sur l'origine, les progrès, et le genre des Romans" in *Toni et Clairette* (Paris, 1773), I, xxiv. And the French continued to read translated English fiction. In "Les Enseignements des bibliothèques privées (1750–1780)," *Revue d'Histoire Littéraire de la France*, XVII (juillet-septembre 1910), 449–496, Daniel Mornet ascertained that out of the ten novels most frequently possessed, five were translations from the English; and they ranked second through sixth in order of popularity.

14. Two works which deal particularly with this social point of view are Daniel Mornet, *La Pensée française au XVIIIᵉ siècle* (Paris: A. Colin, 1938), and Arthur J. Wilson, Jr., "Sensibility in France in the Eighteenth Century: A Study in Word History," *French Quarterly*, XIII (January-June 1931), 35–46.

15. Letter of 2 Janvier 1772 in *The Private Correspondence of David Garrick with the most Celebrated Persons of his Time* (London: H. Colburn and R. Bentley, 1832), II, 595.

16. Statistics on the numerous charitable establishments can be found in Paul Lacroix, *XVIIIᵉ Siècle, institutions, usages et costumes* (Paris: Didot frères, fils et cie, 1875). As to the anthologies, *Les Annales de la bienfaisance*

lard d'Arnaud paid most effusive tribute "à la sensibilité, à cette compassion générale, devenue, si l'on peut le dire, de *mode* parmi nous, grâce à l'exemple de nos augustes Souverains, et à l'heureux enthousiasme qui porte tout Français à les imiter!"[17] A less *sensible* critic remarked, perhaps ironically, "Si notre siècle n'est pas celui où il y a le plus de vertus, c'est du moins celui où l'on fait le mieux les mettre au jour."[18]

Authors, buoyed by critical support and anxious to respond to an eager public, produced a steady stream of sentimental fiction during the last four decades of the century. Two names and two novels stand head and shoulders above the crowd: Jean-Jacques Rousseau and *Julie ou la nouvelle Héloïse* (1761); Bernardin de St.-Pierre and *Paul et Virginie* (1788). To pair the writers thus is fitting, for the first, whose work met with immediate success, established language and content which were to be imitated by countless less talented sentimental writers; and the second, perhaps without knowing it, achieved a synthesis of sentimentality so perfect that no subsequent author approached, let alone equalled, it.[19]

Rousseau's epistolary novel tells of the virtuous Julie d'Etange, whose passion for her tutor St.-Preux leads to her dishonor and his banishment; who experiences, during her marriage ceremony, a total repentance which permits her to regard the past without

---

(1773), *Anecdotes de la bienfaisance* (1777), and *Les Etrennes de la vertu* (1783) are typical titles; and the *Journal de Littérature, des Sciences et des Arts* proclaimed itself to be *au Profit de la Maison d'Institution des jeunes Orphelins militaires. Sous les Auspices du Roi et de la Reine, Protecteurs de cet Etablissement.*

17. *Délassemens de l'homme sensible, ou anecdotes diverses,* IV (Paris, 1783), 239–240.

18. *Histoire de la république des lettres et arts en France: année 1783* (Amsterdam et Paris, 1785), p. 9.

19. The major critical works all, of course, pay considerable attention to these two writers and their importance. For other useful information on Rousseau, see Daniel Mornet, "Introduction" to *La Nouvelle Héloïse,* ed. "Grands Ecrivains de France," Vol. I (Paris: Hachette, 1925), and Charles Dédéyan, *Jean-Jacques Rousseau et la sensibilité littéraire à la fin du XVIIIe siècle* (Paris: S.E.D.E.S., 1966); for a thorough historical and critical analysis of St.-Pierre's work, see Pierre Trahard's introduction to his edition of *Paul et Virginie* (Paris: Classiques Garnier, 1964).

shame and the future with confidence in her virtue; who creates for her family a rural, domestic utopia at Clarens which St.-Preux is invited to join; and who dies, secure in the knowledge of duty accomplished but apprehensive of a future in which her love for St.-Preux might revive. Of all the ideas which became commonplaces of sentimental fiction, three deserve particular mention because of the importance Rousseau gave them. First, *sensibilité*, which St.-Preux calls "un fatal présent du ciel," is constantly at war with reason and may cause one untold grief; but its possession is essential, for it remains, always, the mainspring of virtue. Second, sincere repentance like Julie's can erase all previous faults; one's virtue is not simply restored but reborn. Third, civilized, conventional society is the enemy of happiness, which can best be found by living modestly according to the dictates of nature. The eloquence of Rousseau's prose undoubtedly persuaded his audience to accept these concepts as successfully as it convinced them of the sincerity of the lovers' passion.

The brevity and simplicity of *Paul et Virginie* indicate immediately how much the sentimental novel had developed since 1761. Two mothers, exiled from society to the Ile de France (Mauritius), raise their children together in perfect harmony with nature. At the very moment when their childish companionship becomes unspoken love, Virginie is sent back to France and civilization, and Paul is left to comfort the mothers and bear the sadness of her absence. Virginie returns, but she is drowned in a storm before she can set foot on the island. Paul dies of a broken heart. It is an uncomplicated story which has much in common with *La Nouvelle Héloïse*, but the differences are instructive. Switzerland was a wild and majestic—but still European—setting for Rousseau; St.-Pierre chooses a remote, exotic, tropical isle. Julie and St.-Preux were educated people; Paul and Virginie, who grow up without any formal education, preserve thereby a moral superiority founded on innocence. In the first novel, Julie established a civilized society, albeit a pleasantly rural one, at Clarens; any society larger than the family, and civilization in general, is pernicious in the second. *La Nouvelle Héloïse* shows passion consummated but innocence regained; Virginie's opportune demise begs the question. But like his predecessor, St.-Pierre was a master of style; and the simplicity of plot and characterization was more than enhanced by rich and glowing prose.

The year 1761 saw not only the success of *La Nouvelle Héloïse* but also the enormous popularity of a slender collection of short stories: the *Contes moraux* of Jean-François Marmontel.[20] The first dated in fact from 1758, when Marmontel was attempting to enliven the prosy pages of the *Mercure de France*, of which he was editor; he chose as his general formula a playful moral dilemma which could easily be resolved by a last-minute—and often artificial—appeal to sentiment. His titles often summarize the situations succinctly: "L'Amitié à l'épreuve" culminates with Blandford's generous surrender of his Indian fiancée to his best friend, for instance, and the heroine of "La Femme comme il y en a peu" recovers her ruined husband's fortune by clever domestic management. So successful were his *contes moraux* that they established a brand-new genre; a host of imitators followed in his footsteps, and *contes, romans, fictions, anecdotes,* and *histoires moraux* and *morales* proliferated.[21] Two other works, both within the sentimental genre, gained Marmontel further celebrity. *Bélisaire* (1767) thinly disguised its theories on good government, the education of princes, and religion with a novel-like structure. *Les Incas, ou la destruction de l'Empire du Pérou* (1777) provided its audience

20. Marmontel's *Mémoires*, ed. Maurice Tourneux (Paris: Librairie des bibliophiles, 1891) furnish his own account of his successful career; a modern study is S. Lenel, *Un Homme de lettres au XVIIIe siècle: Marmontel* (Paris: Hachette, 1902). Michelle Buchanan has studied the *contes* separately in "Les *Contes moraux* de Marmontel," *French Review*, XLI (November 1967), 201–212.

21. His most successful imitator was Bricaire de la Dixmérie, his successor on the *Mercure*, who produced his own *Contes moraux et philosophiques* in 1765; others included Contant d'Orville and his *Romans moraux* (1768), *Contes moraux* by both Mlle Uncy (1762–63) and Mme Le Prince de Beaumont (1774), and *Fictions morales* by Mercier as late as 1792. Marmontel himself published another series of *contes* between 1790 and 1793, but they were greeted with tolerance rather than enthusiasm—time was passing him by.

with more sentimental fare; for its earnest plea for religious tolerance was nicely balanced by the love story of the Spaniard Alonzo and Cora, the Peruvian Virgin of the Sun.

Scarcely less popular than Marmontel, but in a different genre, was François-Thomas de Baculard d'Arnaud, the acknowledged dean of the *larmoyant* and *sombre* school of sentimental fiction.[22] Through six volumes of *Les Epreuves du sentiment* (1772–79), four of *Les Nouvelles historiques* (1774–83), and twelve of *Délassemens de l'homme sensible* (1783–87), he harrowed his readers with tales of love betrayed, virtue tormented, and benevolence ignored—until a finale in which the evil-doer repented and reformed. He had his imitators, too; though frequently they wrote no more than one or two works, they faithfully copied and sometimes surpassed his melodramatic plots and declamatory style.[23] Most noteworthy among them and most prolific was no doubt Loaisel de Tréogate, whose works bore such enticing titles as *Les Soirées de mélancholie* (1777) and *Dolbreuse, ou l'homme du siècle ramené à la vérité par le sentiment et par la raison* (1771).[24]

Women novelists brought to sentimental fiction a more restrained and didactic manner. Highest esteem went to Mme Riccoboni, who began her celebrated career in 1758; she always, however, remained something of an anomaly, for although she

22. D'Arnaud was responsible, in fact, for one of the earliest true sentimental novels: *Les Epoux malheureux*, published in 1745, went through over sixty editions by 1785. The three principal sources on his life and works are Bertran de la Villehervé, *François-Thomas de Baculard d'Arnaud: son théâtre et ses théories dramatiques* (Paris: Champion, 1920) ; Charles Monselet, *Les Oubliés et les dédaignés* (Paris: Poulet-Malassis et de Broise, 1861), II, 157–172; and Derk Inklaar, *François-Thomas de Baculard d'Arnaud, ses imitateurs en Hollande et dans d'autres pays* (Gravenhage: De Nederlandsche Boek-en Steendrukkerij, 1925).

23. For example, Nicolas Léonard, *Lettres de deux amans, habitans de Lyon* (1783), Claude Joseph Dorat, *Les Malheurs de l'inconstance* (1772), Constant de Rebècque, *Laure, ou Lettres de quelques femmes de Suisse* (1786), and Mme Daubenton, *Zélie dans le désert* (1786–87).

24. Although little noticed by eighteenth-century French critics, he has received considerable attention from twentieth-century literary historians—Coulet and Etienne in particular—who see in him an important precursor of romantic thought and style.

involved her *sensible* heroines in the most delicate romantic situations, her tone stayed light and her attitude objective rather than self-indulgent.[25] Mme Le Prince de Beaumont was more typical of the feminine sentimentalists, for she preached without respite that virtue would be honored and benevolence recompensed.[26] Also typical and exceedingly successful was Mme de Genlis, who knew how to skillfully combine the morally piquant with a healthy dose of didacticism for the benefit of her readers, in works like *Adèle et Théodore, ou lettres sur l'éducation* (1782) and *Les Veillées du château* (1782).[27]

Below the names of celebrated authors and authoresses of the time stretched a vast list of professional and amateur writers who tried their hand at sentimental fiction and who occasionally had the good fortune to please the public with one or two novels. Gaspard de Beaurieu and *L'Elève de la nature* (1763); Mme Elie de Beaumont and *Lettres du marquis de Roselle* (1764); St.-Lambert and "Sara Th . . . " (1765); Dubois-Fontanelle and *Les Effets des passions* (1786) and *Naufrage et aventures de M. Pierre Viaud* (1768); Claude Joseph Dorat and *Les Sacrifices de l'amour* (1771) and *Les Malheurs de l'inconstance* (1772); Mme de Montolieu and *Caroline de Litchfield* (1786)—all enjoyed brief periods of popularity. That so many writers should have considered

25. Her most popular work, *Lettres de Milady Juliette Catesby* (1759), went through sixteen editions by 1785, proving that she did in fact appeal to a sentimental audience. The only full-length study of her is by Emily A. Crosby, *Une Romancière oubliée, Mme Riccoboni: sa vie, ses oeuvres, sa place dans la littérature anglaise et française du XVIIIe siècle* (Paris: Rieder et cie, 1924).

26. Witness the titles of some of her works: the early *Triomphe de la vérité* (1748); *Mémoires de Madame la baronne de Batteville, ou la veuve parfaite* (1766); *La Nouvelle Clarice* (1767). In addition she found time for moral treatises like *Magasin des enfans, ou dialogues d'une sage gouvernante avec ses élèves de la première distinction*, which was printed nine times between 1758 and 1780.

27. Mme de Genlis was also her own biographer: see her *Mémoires inédits de Mme la comtesse de Genlis*. 10 vols. (Paris: Ladvocat, 1825); the most recent study of her life and works is that by Alice Laborde, *L'Oeuvre de Mme de Genlis* (Paris: Nizet, 1966). Other representative feminine sentimentalists were Fanny de Beauharnais, Mme de Souza, Mme de Montolieu, and Mme de Charrière.

sentimental fiction a genre worth trying at least once indicates the attraction that sentimental novels and stories held for the French reading public for nearly forty years.

It was inevitable, of course, that its attraction should wane. Responsibility for its demise may be laid to three factors, the first of which was, simply, its own degeneration. During the late 1770's, it began to lose the simplicity, sincerity, and straightforwardness which had generally characterized it, as authors realized that they stood in danger of boring their audience irretrievably if they did not offer something more stimulating. So they pushed sentimentalism to its limits: their plots grew more and more extravagant and the moral dilemmas more and more questionable; their characters vacillated wildly between hope and despair; their prose consisted of lamentations, entreaties, and exclamation marks. Such excessive sentimentality did succeed in holding the public's attention through the eighties and early nineties; but it represented a dead end to further development.

Other authors, more adventurous, tacitly accepted sentimentality but groped for newer approaches. Realism, a desire to describe social conditions as they were and not as the sentimentalists thought they should be presented, preoccupied some, like Restif de la Bretonne and Louvet de Couvrai.[28] Escapism, an impulse to retreat into a world still simpler and more pure than that of ordinary sentimental fiction, motivated others—hence chivalric tales, such as those compiled by Legrand d'Aussy, and pastorals like those of the Chevalier de Florian. Literary confusion was the inevitable result of these divergent efforts.[29]

28. Although Louvet de Couvrai also produced the super-sentimental *Emilie de Varmont, ou le divorce nécessaire* (1791).

29. A minor author like Jean Claude Gorjy well demonstrates both the exhaustion of sentimental fictional conventions and the new efforts at experimentation. In *Blançay* (1788), the bourgeois milieu is realistically described but the plot is encumbered by the usual near-rapes, lovers united, and fortunes restored. The hero of *St. Alme* (1790) is in love with Joséphine; but tormented by jealousy on hearing of her marriage, he goes mad and rapes her, only to discover that she has, fortunately, become a widow. *Lidorie* (1790) belongs to

But what doubtless killed sentimental fiction was the French Revolution itself. Novels and stories had been preaching for years that *sensibilité* would inspire good works, beneficial to all mankind; that following natural impulse would lead directly to *liberté, égalité, fraternité*. So, indeed, it seemed during the first years of the Revolution. But as the political situation grew less and less certain and instances of terror and repression more and more frequent, the tenets of sentimentalism collapsed in the face of revolutionary reality and the need to maintain power. "N'aie de l'humanité que pour ta patrie," counseled one writer, *"Oublie que la Nature te fit homme et sensible."*[30] Literature could no longer continue to celebrate what so evidently did not exist: sentimental fiction truly perished when the world for which it had been created disappeared.

---

troubadour fiction; *Tablettes sentimentales du bon Pamphile* (1791) is an attempt at a pastoral.

30. Quoted by Pierre Trahard, *La Sensibilité révolutionnaire (1789–1794)* (Paris: Boivin et cie, 1936), p. 91, who chronicles this evolution particularly in chapters 3 and 4.

CHAPTER TWO. THE COMMERCIAL VENTURE

To talk of literature purely as a commercial venture may seem somewhat restrictive; but, in the case of the vogue for translated French sentimental fiction in late eighteenth-century England, it provides a useful way to approach the phenomenon as a whole. It obliges one to look closely at the interests of the two groups—leaving aside, for the present, the public—which sustained the genre's popularity: the publishers and the translators. It requires one to analyze why they thought such translations might be a successful commercial enterprise. And it demands that one prove with data and statistics whether those involved were right or wrong in their suppositions; in this case, as will be seen, they were most certainly right.

The chief question for publisher and translator alike was, of course, would translated sentimental novels sell? or, to phrase it more accurately, did this foreign fiction have qualities that would appeal to the British public, and were times favorable for its introduction and continuation? After that, their interests diverged. The publisher had to consider the financial aspects: how much he would pay to whom for the finished product. The translator had, besides the financial prospects, practical and esthetic concerns: how he would choose what he translated; how he would deal with "foreign" fiction in the light of prevailing British taste; what his responsibilities to the French original and to his audience might be.

If a prospective translator or publisher was hesitant about putting French fiction before the public, he might well have reflected that such foreign translations had long been a part of the literary fare offered to British readers. During the seventeenth century the heroic romances had been translated into English almost as soon as they appeared, sometimes in more than one version, and they often ran through several editions.[1] No decade from 1700 to 1760

1. For example, John Davis translated Madeleine de Scudéry's *Clélie* in five

went by without a number of importations from abroad; and works of writers like Scarron, Le Sage, Mme d'Aulnoy, le chevalier de Mouhy, Marivaux, Prévost, and Crébillon *fils*, to name only the more prominent, were readily available.[2] The act of translating or publishing was not, therefore, either so new or so unusual as to frighten the timid.

Prospective translators and booksellers might have drawn equal encouragement from the fact that British readers were curious about contemporary literature across the channel. That this curiosity was deliberately fostered is no doubt likely. Nevertheless, it is worth noting that throughout the last decades of the century, important English critical journals made a practice of reviewing French novels in the original language before translations of them were available in England. The three major successes in France circa 1760—*La Nouvelle Héloïse*, Marmontel's *Contes moraux*, and Mme Riccoboni's *Lettres de Milady Juliette Catesby*—received immediate attention; works by Baculard d'Arnaud, Mme de Genlis, and the Chevalier de Florian were also noticed and commended.[3]

---

volumes, 1655–61, which coincided with the work's appearance in France; George Havers produced a similarly lengthy version in 1677–78. The same authoress' *Artamène ou le grand Cyrus* and *Ibrahim* both had two editions; La Calprenède's *Cassandre* was published five times between 1652 and 1676. For complete bibliographical details, see Charles C. Mish, *English Prose Fiction 1600–1700* (Charlottesville: Bibliographical Society of the University of Virginia, 1952).

2. Roughly speaking, eighteen translations appeared from 1700–09; ten from 1710–19; thirty-one from 1720–29; twenty-five from 1730–39; fifty-one from 1740–49; and sixteen from 1750–59. These statistics (and the authors mentioned) are drawn from W. H. McBurney, *A Check List of English Prose Fiction, 1700–1739* (Cambridge: Harvard University Press, 1960), Jerry C. Beasley, *A Check List of Prose Fiction Published in England 1740–49* (Charlottesville: University Press of Virginia, 1972), and Andrew Block, *The English Novel, 1740–1850*, 2nd ed. (London: Dawson, 1961); it should be noted, of course, that they comprise translations of very diverse sorts of fiction—oriental stories, historical romances, picaresque and satiric novels, as well as tales of a romantic nature.

3. *La Nouvelle Héloïse* was reviewed by the *Gentleman's Magazine*, XXXI (January 1761), the *Monthly Review*, XXIII (December 1760), and the *Critical Review*, XI (January 1761); the *Contes moraux* were mentioned by

Public attention was being drawn to French fiction in other ways, too. Many journals ran anecdotes about the more famous French authors. During 1782–83 the *European Magazine and London Review* published "A View of French Literature for the Present Century," a series of brief biographical and critical studies of the prominent contemporary literati. Anthologies of translated stories helped to publicize the foreign writers; in her three-volume *Sketches of the Lives and Writings of the Ladies of France* (1780), for example, Mrs. Thicknesse gave personal histories and extracts of works "for the information and excitement of the English Ladies."[4] Nor did British literary critics and historians neglect French novelists: James Beattie discussed Rousseau in *On Fable and Romance* (1783); and Clara Reeve, who in *The Progress of Romance* (1785) said of the French novels "That the best are the most *excellent*, and the worst the most *execrable* of all others," commented on Prévost, Marivaux, Mme Riccoboni, Rousseau, Marmontel, Mme Elie de Beaumont, and Mme de Genlis.[5]

Past history could reassure the commercial entrepreneurs about the probability of success of translations from the French; contemporary publicity about the foreign sources provided visibility for their productions. But what of the fundamental nature of the

---

an enthusiastic reader in the *Monthly Review*, XXV (December 1761), and Marmontel's *Incas* commented upon in the *London Review*, Appendix (June 1777) and the *Monthly Review*, LVI (March 1777); the Catesby letters were reviewed by the *Critical Review*, IX (January 1760); D'Arnaud's collection *Délassemens de l'homme sensible*, no long story from which ever appeared in English, was discussed in the *Monthly*, LXX (May 1784) and the *European*, IV (December 1783); Mme de Genlis' *Adèle et Théodore* was mentioned in the *Monthly*, LXVI (June 1782) and her *Chevaliers du cygne* in the *Analytical Review*, XXIII (January 1796) and the *Monthly*, 2nd ser., XIX (April 1796); Florian's *Numa Pompilius* was reviewed in the *English Review*, IX (February 1787) and *Gonsalve de Cordoue* in the *Monthly*, 2nd ser., VII (April 1792).

4. *Sketches of the Lives and Writings of the Ladies of France* (London: L. Dodsley and W. Brown, 1780), I, xxi. Robert Watt, in his *Bibliotheca Britannica* (Edinburgh: A. Constable, 1824) indicates two other similar works, which I have not seen: *The Literati of France* (1786) and *The Works of Celebrated French Women* (1786).

5. *The Progress of Romance* (1785; rpt New York: Facsimile Text Society, 1930), I, 128, hereafter cited in the text.

literature in question: was sentimental French fiction likely to attract the British public? The answer was an inescapable affirmative; for during the later decades of the 1700's, the English audience was as interested in sensibility and its attributes as its counterpart across the channel.

Philosophical and theoretical speculations early in the century —those of the Cambridge Platonists, for example, and Lord Shaftesbury—had been preparing a favorable climate for sentimentality in England. In opposition to Hobbes' concept of human nature, opinion began to insist that the heart of man was naturally good and inclined to humanitarian sentiments; disputing the Stoic notion of unemotional benevolence, it praised the pleasures experienced in the performance of kindly acts; and anti-Puritan, it replaced a vengeful deity with a benevolent God and lauded the efficacy of works over doctrinal faith.[6] Reflections of such developments found expression in a work like Adam Smith's *Theory of Moral Sentiments* (1759); and his statement that "the amiable virtue of humanity requires, surely, a sensibility, much beyond what is possessed by the rude vulgar of mankind, a degree of sensibility which surprises by its exquisite and unexpected delicacy and tenderness" already suggested the emotionally aristocratic nature of sentimentality which fiction, both English and French, was to exploit.[7]

During the last decades of the century, panegyrics to sentiment multiplied in periodicals and books; Hannah More's effusion, though poetical, is representative—

6. The following works offer thorough studies of the points mentioned in the historical development of English sensibility: R. S. Crane, "Suggestions toward a Genealogy of the 'Man of Feeling,'" *ELH*, I (December 1934), 205–230; Louis Bredvold, *The Natural History of Sensibility* (Detroit: Wayne State University Press, 1962), pp. 1–26; Lois Whitney, *Primitivism and the Idea of Progress in English Popular Literature of the Eighteenth Century* (Baltimore: Johns Hopkins, 1934), particularly pp. 91–136; and James R. Warner, " 'Education of the Heart': Observations on the Eighteenth-Century English Sentimental Movement," *Papers of the Michigan Academy of Science, Arts, and Letters*, XXIX (1943), 553–560.

7. *The Theory of Moral Sentiments*, 3rd ed. (London, 1767), p. 33.

> Sweet Sensibility! thou keen delight!
> Unprompted moral! sudden sense of right!
> Perception exquisite! fair virtue's seed!
> Thou quick precursor of the lib'ral deed!
> Thou hasty conscience! reason's blushing morn!
> Instinctive kindness e'er reflexion's born![8]

Moreover, enthusiasts emphasized that sensibility was an integral element of literature. The study of "Poets and Sentimental Writers," said one partisan, "contributes more than all other causes to humanize the heart, and refine the sentiments."[9] Like the French critics, they demanded that the novel, in addition to furnishing instruction, appeal as well to the reader's emotions while doing so. Clara Reeve was not concerned with the intellectual when she asked that in fiction, "Virtue should always be represented in the most beautiful and amiable light, capable of attracting the *hearts* of her votaries, and of rewarding every sacrifice they can make to her" (II, 27; italics mine).

Alert eyes would have had little trouble discerning as well that the criticism of English reviewers was mediating, to their commercial advantage, between this esteem for sensibility and the talents of French sentimental writers. Those advance reviewers, even in 1760, stressed that situations involving sentiment and delicacy of feeling formed an important part of the foreign novels and that they were handled with the utmost skill and perceptivity.[10] Some later critics insisted, in fact, that French authors were superior to the English in this respect.[11] Sentimental novels, main-

---

8. "Traits of Sensibility. From Sensibility, a Poetical Epistle. By Miss H. More," *Universal Magazine*, LXX (February 1782), 98, a work also affixed to her *Sacred Dramas* (1782). R. W. Babcock provides a list of late eighteenth-century effusions on sensibility in "Benevolence, Sensibility, and Sentiment in Some Eighteenth-Century Periodicals," *MLN*, LXII (June 1947), 394–97.

9. "On Delicacy of Sentiment," *Universal*, LXII (April 1778), 173.

10. The reviewer of the *Critical*, in his notice of Kenrick's translation of *La Nouvelle Héloïse*, specifically compared the French work to *Clarissa* and preferred the former, which he found "infinitely more sentimental, animated, refined, and elegant": XII (September 1761), 205.

11. The *English Review* thus praised Mme de Genlis' *Adelaide and Theo-*

tained Henry Mackenzie, "have been borrowed from our neighbours the French, whose style of manners, and the very powers of whose language give them a great advantage in the delineations of that nicety, that subtility of feelings, those entanglements of delicacy which are so much interwoven with the characters and conduct of the chief personages in many of their most celebrated novels."[12] The *English Review* even declared that "The French are, without exception, the best novelists in the world. They have a great deal of fancy, sensibility, volatility, and versatility, with a happy way of expressing themselves; qualities almost essential to make a novel pleasing."[13]

The evidence presented regarding the long-standing status of translated French fiction, the curiosity about contemporary foreign authors, and, most particularly, the prevailing passion for sentimentality during the period is hopefully sufficient to indicate that enterprising translators and publishers could well afford to gamble that translations of French sentimental novels and stories would be highly marketable to the English reading public. It is the modern literary historian, however, who is best able to perceive how propitious times were for such translations; for after the death of Smollett in 1771, fiction in England became the province of second- and third-rate authors for thirty years.[14] A few well-constructed and interesting novels did appear; some authors were clearly more talented than others. But the majority of works were mediocre in style and content, and the novelists were content to rehash themes

---

dore: "The work is full of *sentiment*, but of a very different kind from that affectation of unfelt sympathy which enters into the composition of English novels . . . [and we give] the author a higher rank in merit than we are disposed to bestow on *sentimentalists* of our own nation": II (August 1783), 106–107.

12. *The Lounger*, No. 20, 18 June 1785, pp. 78–79.

13. *English Review*, VII (September 1786), 184.

14. This period is thoroughly discussed by J. M. S. Tompkins in her distinguished study *The Popular Novel in England, 1770–1800* (1932; rpt Lincoln: University of Nebraska Press, 1961); acknowledging that the fiction was "tenth-rate," she nevertheless emphasizes that it "fed the appetite of the reading public, [and] reflected and shaped their imaginations" (p. v).

familiar from the works of their four illustrious predecessors for a public that welcomed fiction openheartedly and indiscriminately.

This sort of literary vacuum was ideally suited for the introduction of translations of French sentimental fiction. No major English novelist then working could be held up as a standard against which to measure the French writers—and French literature had, after all, one major novelist to offer in Rousseau. Esteemed authors like Marmontel, Mme Riccoboni, Baculard d'Arnaud, and Mme de Genlis were at least the equals of the second-line English writers; and the mass of anonymous or nearly anonymous foreign authors were no worse than their British counterparts. Translations from the French could thus simply "slip in" on the English literary scene, not as challengers to the indigenous fiction but rather as legitimate competitors for public favor.

There is a third way to phrase that initial question of publishers and translators, "Will French sentimental fiction sell?"—namely, "Is there a public available to read these translations?" Early in the 1700's the novel-reading public was small but growing; during the second half of the century it began to increase by (relatively speaking) leaps and bounds.[15] Obviously, those people—particularly the ladies—who read volumes of English fiction with great enjoyment would be likely to take equal pleasure in translated sentimental novels. They did not even have to buy them. They could borrow them from the multiplying number of libraries, public, private, and circulating, upon payment of a small fee.

But another public was waiting to be tapped as well: the magazine readers. English periodicals, which had been carrying fiction since the late 1600's, began to add even more during the second half of the eighteenth century, particularly after 1770.[16] Short

15. A. S. Collins describes the growth of the novel-reading public in *Authorship in the Days of Johnson* (London: Robert Halden, 1927), pp. 232–258; see also Ian Watt, *The Rise of the Novel* (Berkeley: University of California Press, 1957), pp. 35–49.

16. Information about English magazines of the period has been largely gathered from Robert Mayo, *The English Novel in the Magazines, 1740–1815* (Evanston: Northwestern University Press, 1962); this indispensable work

stories were tucked into one or two issues; longer works were serialized over a period of months or even years. Depending on the prestige of the magazines, the novels and stories might reach as many as 15,000 subscribers a month. Much French sentimental fiction was ideally suited to magazine publication from the standpoint of length alone. The enormous success of the *conte moral* (which, it should be remembered, had originally been written for a French periodical) provided a reservoir of brief material on which to draw; the *nouvelle*, slightly longer than the *conte*, was still of manageable size for serialization. To the novel-reading public was thus added another public of considerable size, waiting to be furnished with foreign translations.

Publishers and translators alike shared a common interest in the appeal of French sentimental fiction to the British public, the proper timing of its appearance, and the availability of a reading public. After that, their interests diverged, and it is not improbable that financial considerations—specifically, how much to pay to whom—were uppermost in the publishers' minds.

The editor of a magazine had considerably fewer problems in this respect than the bookseller who was printing regular volumes. Besides his usual staff, he could count on amateurs who were willing to forego pay for the pleasure of seeing their efforts in print to contribute some translated fiction; the *Lady's Magazine* in particular relied for original translations on eager debutantes like "Harriot Delany, a young lady of nineteen" and "Miss Georgiana H——t, a young lady between sixteen and seventeen." If enough contributions were not forthcoming, he could borrow from already published anthologies of translated fiction: Mrs. Thicknesse's *Sketches of the Lives and Writings of the Ladies of France* (1780) and *Tales, Romances, Apologues, Anecdotes, and Novels* (1786) were well mined by the periodicals.[17] If times were truly lean, he

---

contains, as well as history and bibliography, an appendix on foreign fiction in translation (pp. 370–381) which summarizes general trends in the popularity of important foreign authors like Marmontel, D'Arnaud, and Florian.

17. Three stories from the latter appeared in the *Lady's Magazine*. The

could reprint translations featured in other magazines: provincial journals frequently entertained their readers in this way.[18] The editors' reluctance to pay for material they might get gratis no doubt accounts for the fact that no significant contemporary author ever provided a complete original translation for a British periodical.[19]

The booksellers, however, were obliged to pay someone; and although it is very difficult to acquire precise information about their financial practices, a few details are worth mentioning.[20] Very likely, they paid translators directly for the work they turned in as though it were their own. The going rate for original fiction was anywhere from half a guinea per volume for novels in manuscript to twenty pounds, depending on the liberality of the bookseller, and probably payments to translators seldom exceeded the latter figure.[21] It is not clear whether translations were frequently com-

---

former furnished material for the *Universal*, the *London Magazine*, and the *Lady's*, among others; in fact, although the original *Inès de Cordoue* (1696) by Mlle Bernard was a rather classical love story typical of its period, Mrs. Thicknesse's updated translation suited late eighteenth-century taste so well that it was reprinted at least eight times by 1800—hence its inclusion as a sentimental translation.

18. To take a typical example: the *Universal* published an original translation from D'Arnaud, "The Lord of Crequi," in October-November 1782 and January 1783; it was promptly picked up by the *Caledonian Magazine and Review* (1783), and later tapped by the *New London* (1786), the *Gentleman's and London* (1786), and the *Berwick Museum* (1786-87).

19. The only original translator of any importance for the periodicals was "the Author of *The Old English Baron*," Clara Reeve, who furnished the beginning of Lamarche-Courmont's *Letters of Aza* to the *Lady's* in June-July 1778, then abruptly refused to continue despite anguished editorial pleas to "Miss Clara"; Mayo, who relates the incident in detail, speculates that she suddenly realized that the *Lady's* intended to capitalize on her reputation without any financial reward for her and decided to have no part of such an arrangement.

20. Collins, in the work already cited and in *The Profession of Letters* (New York: Dutton, 1929), discusses payments made to established authors; but because he is primarily interested in major figures like Johnson, Hawkesworth, and Goldsmith, the sums he mentions were probably the exception rather than the rule. In addition, Watt (pp. 52–59) emphasizes the importance and the economic power of the booksellers in determining the kinds of literature produced.

21. Thomas Rees, in *Reminiscences of Literary London, from 1779 to 1853* (London: Suckling and Galloway, 1896), states that William Lane paid his

missioned, but there is at least one instance of it. When Thomas Holcroft went to France in 1783, the publisher Rivington "engaged in an agreement, or adventure with Mr. Holcroft, that works were to be selected, and translated by him, and published for their joint and equal account, he (Mr. Rivington) advancing money to Mr. Holcroft [one and a half guineas a week is mentioned elsewhere], as a loan for his expenses."[22] Holcroft turned up Mme de Genlis' *Les Veillées du château* and Billardon de Sauvigny's *Pierre le Long*, but for some unexplained reason, the translations were published by Robinson instead.

Whereas payment to the English translator was a fact, payment to the French author was a delicate question of ethics, often conveniently ignored. There seems to have been no question of reciprocal copyright; the fiction lay there to be plundered at will, as indeed it was. One might wonder whether the most celebrated authors who knew about the foreign popularity of their works were annoyed at realizing nothing from them, but Marmontel, Rousseau, and Mme de Genlis say nothing in their memoirs or correspondence about their feelings on the subject.[23] The one glimpse into an

authors from ten to twenty pounds for novels. The figure of half a guinea per volume comes from James Lackington, himself the first large-volume second-hand bookseller, who continues, "it is a shocking price, to be sure, but it should be remembered that as there are some of the trade who are mean enough to wish to obtain valuable copy-rights for nothing; so, on the other hand, many novels have been offered to booksellers; indeed, many have actually been published, that were not worth the expence of paper and printing, so that the copyright was dear at any price": *Memoirs of the Forty-Five First Years of the Life of James Lackington*, 13th ed. (London: Printed for and sold by the Author, 1791), p. 235.

22. *Memoirs of the Late Thomas Holcroft, written by himself*, ed. W. C. Hazlitt (London: Longman, Hurst, et al, 1816), II, 44. Similar interest on the part of publishers is described by John Nichols in *Literary Anecdotes of the Eighteenth Century*, VIII (London: Printed for the author, 1814), 24: Percival Stockdale had completed a translation of Tasso's *Aminta* for David in 1770, "Drs. Johnson and Hawkesworth gave the translator their warm approbation; and it attracted to the shrine of his Muse many of the London Booksellers" who came bearing commissions.

23. Marmontel in his *Mémoires* mentions the enormous European success of his *Bélisaire*—40,000 volumes sold in a few months—but is chiefly delighted because such general acclaim afforded him protection against the attacks of

English bookseller's transactions with a French author comes from Mme Riccoboni's letters to David Garrick, whom she kept apprised of her dealings with Becket. If the French bookseller had bought and published the manuscript, she had no right to royalties in France but might make a profit if an English bookseller purchased copies of the French edition and sold them in London; so it would seem from her report that Becket had asked her for one hundred copies of *Lettres d'Adelaide de Dammartin, comtesse de Sancerre* (1767), fifty for him, fifty for her "dont je souhaite d'être payée."[24] If, however, a manuscript had been printed at her expense and all French profits belonged to her, the matter altered, as in the case of her *Lettres de Elisabeth-Sophie de Vallière* (1771). Garrick took charge of its translation into English, chose Mackinnon (or Maceuen) to produce it for Becket, and arranged that the profits should go to Mme Riccoboni. It soon became clear, however, that the translation was not selling, due possibly to derogatory remarks about it in an influential journal, and she received nothing until February 1773. Then, she happily wrote Garrick, Becket sent her an apologetic letter and twenty pounds—evidently because he had received a thorough scolding from Garrick himself —and further proposed that he buy the rights to *Elisabeth-Sophie*

the church. In Rousseau's *Correspondance générale*, ed. Th. Dufour et P. Plan (Paris: A. Colin, 1924–34), there is only one letter from William Kenrick, dated September 1766, who identifies himself as "The translator of Eloisia [sic], Emilius, etc.," announces a project to publish Rousseau's complete works, and solicits from him an autobiography. Rousseau's answer is quite indifferent: "quant à leur publication en anglois que vous m'annoncez, je n'y prends d'autre interest que celui de désirer qu'elle vous soit avantageuse. Je n'entends gêner vos libraires en aucune sorte" (XXVI, 72). Mme de Genlis is no more communicative on the subject. In the ten volumes of her *Mémoires inédits* (Paris: Ladvocat, 1825), her only reference to her popularity abroad is a remark that "M. Emsly [sic], libraire à Londres, m'a dit en avoir fait, dans l'espace de deux ans, vingt-deux éditions françoises" of *Les Veillées du château* (III, 189–190) ; yet she knew Holcroft personally and corresponded with him.

24. Letter of 14 Novembre 1767, *The Private Correspondence of David Garrick with the Most Celebrated Persons of his Time* (London: H. Colburn and R. Bentley, 1832), II, 525. Earlier letters indicate that she had made similar arrangements before, taking out profits in English books rather than cash.

for twenty louis and take full charge of the edition, an arrangement which she accepted.[25] Garrick's kindness in the matter was exceptional, and since few French authors could boast such a distinguished English friend, very likely the situation was unique.

If the financial considerations involved in publishing book-length translations of French sentimental fiction differed little, for the booksellers, from their customary practices, the translators who operated in that literary market found the situation equally to their benefit. Translations were in demand, and publishers were not overly scrupulous about the quality of the translations they put out.[26] Translating presented, in fact, one great advantage: it did not require as much time and effort as an original piece of fiction. That this was the case is indicated by the number of professional authors, generally women, who alternately produced translations of French novels and their own original works.[27] Payment was adequate; and if the translator were very enterprising, he could first seek out subscribers to guarantee the initial success of his work

25. The history of this transaction is recorded in the letters of 24 Septembre 1771, 2 Janvier 1772, 12 Janvier 1773, and 3 Février 1773. The campaign against the translation she had on hearsay from a friend; but it is true that the *Monthly Review*, XLI (July 1772), although praising the work in general, condemned the translation as without "propriety or force" and cited parallel passages to prove it.

26. Mr. Tooke, who bemoaned cheap translations "finished and hurried through the press in the space of six weeks," quoted the excuses of a bookseller "that 'the public curiosity is screwed to its highest pitch, and must be gratified; and that to provide a better translation would demand a greater expence of time and money, without procuring the sale of one additional copy' ": cited by John Nichols, IX (London, 1815), 172.

27. This state of affairs existed, of course, before 1760, a prime example being Eliza Haywood, who busied herself with both translations and original fiction in the 1720's and 1730's. Sarah Scott, authoress of several minor novels in the fifties and sixties and translator of La Place's *Laideur aimable* in 1754, confirms it in a letter to her sister: "I have likewise another favor to ask which is a great secret . . . You often have french novels before they become common, if you coud help me to any, a time spent in translating woud turn much to my profit, if I coud get a translation done before any other had publish'd one." This is quoted by Gaby E. Onderwyzer in "Sarah Scott's *Agreeable Ugliness*, A Translation," *MLN*, LXX (December 1955), 579.

and then sell the copyright to an interested bookseller for an additional sum.[28]

To profit from the financial possibilities offered by book-length translations, however, the translator had to make that first crucial —and, hopefully, shrewd—decision: what work by which French author to offer to the British public. Although each was no doubt privately influenced in his choice by considerations of saleability, a number took the opportunity to explain their selections publicly in prefaces and advertisements. Persuasively, they sought both to justify their presentations and to coax the reluctant reader into taking an interest in their work.

Sometimes the celebrity of the author, at home or abroad, furnished a pretext for translation. Sophia Lee declared, concerning D'Arnaud's *Varbeck*, that "the general approbation which his productions have received from his own countrymen, induced a presumption that a subject purely English, from so eminent a pen, would not be unacceptable to an English reader."[29] "The genius of M. Marmontel has been of late so much admired in this kingdom," explained the translator of *Belisarius*, "that a work from his pen could not but attract the most early attention."[30] If the author was known to be particularly virtuous or benevolent, this fact might add luster to a translation. The life of Mme de Graffigny prefixed to the 1771 edition of *The Peruvian Letters* praised "The distinguishing marks of her character [which are] a sensibility, and a goodness of heart, scarcely to be paralleled."[31] The reader of *Charite and Polydorus* (1799) was promised that "The sentiments it inculcates, and the morality it breathes, are likewise such as

28. Precisely what P. S. Dupuy did with his translation from Gorjy, *Sentimental Tablets of the Good Pamphile* (1796), according to Charles Lamb: "As curious a specimen of translation as ever fell into my hands, is a young man's in our office. . . . I had much trouble licking the book into any meaning at all. Yet did the knave clear fifty or sixty pounds by subscription and selling the copyright"—cited in *The Letters of Charles Lamb*, ed. E. V. Lucas (London: Dent, 1935), I, 29.

29. "Preface" to *Warbeck: a pathetic tale* (Dublin, 1786), p. i.

30. *Belisarius* (London, 1767), p. iii.

31. *Letters written by a Peruvian Princess* (London, 1771), p. viii.

might be expected from the pen of the benevolent Barthelemy."[32]

Some translators appealed to the effect their work would have on the reader. Clara Reeve hoped that if her version of D'Arnaud's "D'Almanzi," *The Exiles* (1788), "speaks to the hearts of the generous and the humane, those hearts will become its protectors."[33] The adventures of Pierre Viaud "must necessarily inspire the most timid and desponding mind, with a thorough reliance upon Providence," Mrs. Griffith believed.[34] *Letters Written from Lausanne* (1799), translated from Mme de Charrière, will "everywhere afford innocent amusement to the admirers of simplicity and nature."[35]

Most often, however, the translators emphasized the moral qualities of the fiction they were presenting. Dedicating his translation of Mme Riccoboni's *Letters from Lord Rivers* (1778) to a bishop's wife, Percival Stockdale assured her "that the following Letters, though they form a Novel, deserve the Attention of the Serious, and the Good; that their Authour has given a moral force to Reason, to Sentiment, and to the Passions; which are drawn forth by a Lady (much to the honour of your Sex) under the banner of Virtue."[36] The anonymous translator of the 1792 *Nouveaux Contes moraux* by Marmontel averred that "Few sermons, we believe, will inculcate, with equal success, the practice of virtue, or furnish the mind with more elevated sentiments."[37] Daniel Malthus emphasized "the enlarged views, the pure vein of moral instruction, and the sublime ideas of religion, which characterize the pen of M. de St. Pierre,"

32. *Charite and Polydorus, a romance* (London, 1799), p. vii. A French scholar of considerable repute, Barthélemy was already well known in England for his multi-volume *Voyages du jeune Anacharsis* (1788), translated several years before *Carite et Polydore*.

33. *The Exiles; or, Memoirs of the Count de Cronstadt* (London, 1788), I, xx.

34. *The Shipwreck and Adventures of Monsieur Pierre Viaud* (London, 1771), pp. ix–x.

35. *Letters Written from Lausanne* (Bath, 1799), I, i.

36. *Letters from Lord Rivers to Sir Charles Cardigan* (London, 1778), I, vi.

37. *The Tales of an Evening, followed by The Honest Breton* (London, 1792), p. viii.

in *Paul and Mary* (1789).[38] Thomas Holcroft paid enthusiastic homage "to the eternal honour of Madame de Genlis" whose "enchanting lessons incessantly tend to inspire universal philanthropy; to draw the most amiable, and therefore the most just, pictures of virtue: to soften the asperities of the passions; to teach gentleness, benevolence, fortitude; justice toward ourselves, charity towards others, and to induce that superior, that rational conduct, which alone can generate happiness."[39]

The insistance on the admirable morality inculcated by the translations emphasizes a particular concern of the translators: the possibility of a conservative reaction against fiction which might appear inappropriate or even contrary to British propriety and morality. Critical opinion was disposed to tolerate sensibility in fiction, provided it remained within bounds; but it was wary of sentiment's being overvalued at reason's expense or refined to unnatural extremes. The *Analytical Review* sounded a typical warning: "Hunting after shadows, the moderate enjoyments are despised and its duties neglected; the imagination suffered to stray beyond the utmost verge of probability, where no vestige of nature appears, soon shuts out reason." Sentimental fiction might well have deleterious effects: "the heart is depraved when it is supposed to be refined [by this sort of literature]; and it is a great chance but false sentiment leads to sensuality and vague fabricated feelings supply the place of principles."[40]

38. *Paul and Mary, an Indian Story* (London, 1789), I, vi.

39. *Tales of the Castle*, 3rd ed. (London, 1787), I, i–ii.

40. *Analytical Review*, I (June 1788), 208. Cf. also Henry Mackenzie, who objected to putting "into competition" with ordinary duties and pleasures "the exertions of generosity, of benevolence, and of compassion" as shown in novels, for "even of these virtues of sentiment there are still more refined divisions, in which the over-strained delicacy of the persons represented always leads them to act from the motive least obvious, and therefore generally the least reasonable": *The Lounger*, No. 20, 18 June 1785, p. 79. Similar remonstrances can be found in Kenrick's review of Mistelet's *De la sensibilité* in the *London Review*, V (June 1777), 505–506, and "On Benevolence and Friendship, as Opposed to Principle," in *Essays, by a Society of Gentlemen, at Exeter* (Exeter: Trewman and son, 1796). As Chapter 3 will show, the translators' fears of a conser-

That the translators were conscious of this conservative attitude and did exercise some care in choosing works which would not offend the magazine- or novel-reading public is suggested by the absence or infrequency of translations from certain French authors. British readers were ignorant of Loaisel de Tréogate's melodramatic portrayals of doom and sensuality; nor had they available more than one translated work by notable sentimentalists like Ducray-Duminil, Dorat, Bastide, and Contant d'Orville.[41] The most outstanding example of discretionary selection, however, involved the works of Baculard d'Arnaud serialized in the magazines. A great number of harrowing tales of misfortune like "Valmiers," which shows the distresses of bastardy, or "Nancy," whose heroine gives birth prematurely, is deserted by her husband for her supposed infidelity, and dies in poverty with her child, were to be had for the taking; but translators for the periodicals generally restricted their choices to his sentimental and pathetic domestic or historical fiction, and his gloomy melancholy went almost unknown across the channel.[42]

The translator's concern with suitability by no means ended after he had selected an appropriate work of fiction to present; he was further obliged to consider whether his responsibility as intermediary lay with his foreign original or with the public he

vative reaction to sentimental literature in general were often justified by reviews of their translations.

41. Actually, the British did read a translation from Loaisel de Tréogate, if Daniel Mornet's attribution is correct, two different versions of *Le Fils naturel* entitled *Julius, or the Natural Son* (1789) and *The Natural Son* (1799); but the first was anonymous and the second was ascribed by the translator to Diderot.

42. British novel readers did, however, have a taste of D'Arnaud's *sombre*, for translators who produced book-length versions of his works were somewhat more adventurous. The heroine of Clara Reeve's *The Exiles* (1788), from "D'Almanzi," is raped and later tormented by a villain; and particularly in Sophia Lee's *Warbeck* (1786), there are a number of grisly scenes, including a finale during which Warbeck's wife, who has been living with him in a cave for a number of years, attempts to save her child from soldiers by impaling herself on their swords.

wished to attract. Should he adhere exactly to the French work? Occasionally a translator admitted that he had, like Mrs. Brooke in her version of Framéry's *Memoirs of the Marquis de St. Forlaix* (1770): "The general tendency of this novel to promote the cause of virtue . . . will, she hopes, sufficiently apologize for some exceptional passages . . . which, had she not thought fidelity the first duty of a translator, she would have wished to omit."[43] Or ought he to alter and emend where he felt necessary? The majority of authors who raised the issue unhesitatingly declared yes. "Of the present version [of *Tales of the Castle*], therefore, let it only be observed, it was never intended to be anything like literal," said Thomas Holcroft; "that the phrases are sometimes contracted, and sometimes lengthened; that the liberty of adding a thought is sometimes taken; . . . and that other little freedoms have been taken."[44]

Translators cited various reasons to excuse or justify their license. The basic difficulty of rendering one language into another naturally caused problems. "It will, in some instances, be impossible to reach the delicacy of expression in an elegant French writer," explained William Kenrick in his preface to *Eloisa*; "but, in return, their language is frequently so vague and diffuse, that it must be entirely the fault of the English translator if he does not often improve upon his original; but this will never be the case unless we sit down with a design to translate the *ideas* rather than the *words* of our author."[45] Propriety must be considered. Miss Gunning, for instance, "flatters herself that the trifling alterations she has thought it necessary to make from the original work . . . will meet with indulgence, particularly from her own sex, who certainly cannot be displeased that female delicacy should be preserved in all its purity."[46] And the touchy issue of differing national tastes could not be ignored. Many an English author had little hesitancy in proceeding, like the translator of Florian, "with a license

43. *Memoirs of the Marquis de St. Forlaix* (London, 1770), pp. vii–viii.
44. I, iii.
45. *Eloisa, or a Series of Original Letters*, 4th ed. (London, 1784), I, vii–viii.
46. *Memoirs of Madame Barneveldt* (London, 1795), p. i.

which we think absolutely requisite for the difference of manners existing between French and English readers."[47]

That the translators did use their own judgment in dealing with the foreign originals is proved by differences between the French and English versions of some works. Material evidently considered extraneous to the plot was omitted. Helen Maria Williams admitted that she left out of St.-Pierre's *Paul and Virginia* (1795) "several pages of general observations" on tropical flora and fauna "which, however excellent in themselves, would be passed over with impatience by the English reader, when they interrupt the pathetic narrative."[48] Likewise ignored were the last seventy-five pages of Mme Le Prince de Beaumont's "Le Vrai Point d'honneur," which contained innumerable but irrelevant instances of benevolence and a "Memoir sur les hôpitaux," and the long memorandum on the state of European arts and sciences which terminated Beaurieu's *L'Elève de la nature*. Also judged unnecessary were the French authors' prefaces and footnotes, which generally were not translated. Their omission was, however, more significant than might at first appear, because they often contained the most effusive and extravagant justifications of the writers' moral intentions. Eliminating them protected the British public one step further from immoderate French sentimentality.[49]

47. *Tales, Romances, Apologues, Anecdotes, and Novels* (London, 1786), I, ii. Holcroft made the same point in a letter to Mme de Genlis. Defending his "retrenchments," he explained that "to an English reader I have done the book a service and no injury": *Memoirs*, III, 280. "Truth and nature," he concluded, "are the same in all countries, but the mode of decoration varies in each. — This I hope Madam, will be a sufficient apology for any occasional liberties I may have taken with your very estimable work" (III, 284).

48. *Paul and Virginia* (no imp., 1795), p. vi.

49. An English reader was unaware, for example, that Lavallée intended *Le Nègre comme il y a peu de blancs* (Madras et Paris, 1789) to be impassioned propaganda for "la plus noble des causes, la plus intéressante sans doute que l'on puisse plaider au tribunal de l'humanité . . . celle des Nègres" (I, v) ; or that Beaurieu's object in *L'Elève de la nature* (La Haye et Paris, 1763) was "élever l'homme jusqu'à son Créateur" (I, xiii). In one case, omission of a preface gave the English public precisely the wrong idea of a novel; for Ducray-Duminil explained that his super-sentimental *Alexis ou la maisonette dans les bois* was in fact a satire of the genre.

A more frequent reason for omission was the translator's judgment that certain scenes were too free or too suggestive in the original. Holcroft left out of *Tales of the Castle* a lengthy description of illness and a scene in which a self-sacrificing mother sucks poison from her ailing daughter's eyes "because it is supposed they both would have offended, even violently, the delicacy of an English reader."[50] R. Roberts, in her version of Marmontel's "L'Heureux Divorce," discreetly reduced an amorous encounter with a rake in his mirror-lined boudoir to a few minutes passed in a "lonely closet." James Burne, who admitted that "He found it necessary to suppress some passages" from Beaurieu's *L'Elève de la nature* in *The Man of Nature*, eliminated a scene in which the hero kills a rabbit, finds it pregnant, and, horrified, turns vegetarian.[51]

Once again, it was D'Arnaud's fiction published in the magazines which most definitely indicates censorship. Even in his pathetic stories, scenes involving repentance or death were often considerably shortened; eliminated also were the long moralizing footnotes he provided.[52] The most striking example of expurgation was the translation of "Makin," a tale of horror in which the persecuted lovers flee to Madeira to escape a brutal parent, are shipwrecked, wake in a cavern full of corpses, and finally find peace, after hardship and calamity, with the repentant father. As "The Desert Island, or the Happy Recovery," published in 1778 by the *Universal Magazine*, it was so thoroughly altered by the translator that nothing remained but the unhappy lovers and the happy ending.

With equal freedom the translators added material to make the French originals more appropriate for public consumption. Foot-

50. I, iii.

51. *The Man of Nature* (London, 1773), I, i.

52. "The History of Rosetta," for example, is only the central section of "Clary, ou le retour à la vertu récompensé" and ignores the lover's agonized pursuit of his dishonored mistress whom he finds on her death-bed. "Julia, or the Penitent Daughter" is minus a tearful and benevolent servant, a good deal of anti-middle class sentiment, and a number of footnotes underscoring the moral lessons.

notes were a fashionable technique, perhaps because they offered
the advantage of simultaneously presenting the piquant and moralizing on it. Without omitting Lady Cardigan's spirited defense of
coquetry, Stockdale could still protest that the "conduct here inculcated to young ladies is almost as immoral as the manners of
a Brothel," and hope piously that this note "will prevent any bad
Impressions which might be made by some Passages in these Letters, where Madame Riccoboni authorizes, or very improperly
sports with the mean, and barbarous Arts which are practised by
mistaken, and selfish Women."[53] Other additions were inserted
more directly. Mrs. Griffith supplied another final letter to *The
Fatal Effects of Inconstancy* (1774) to reemphasize the inevita-
bility of the Count's guilty unhappiness. R. Roberts found it necessary to add another whole volume to Mme de Graffigny's *Peruvian
Letters* (1774) because she "was not indeed altogether satisfied
with the conclusion, being desirous the Indian Princess should
become a convert to Christianity through conviction; and that so
generous a friend as Deterville might be as happy as his virtues
deserved."[54]

Despite the numerous assertions that they had endeavored to
make the foreign fiction conform to British mores and taste, however, the translators' emendations and alterations were for the
most part minor.[55] They almost never tampered with the basic plot;

53. II, 97–98. Footnotes chiding authors and characters alike are also supplied in Dorat's *The Fatal Effects of Inconstancy*, Mme de Genlis' *The Rival
Mothers*, and Mme Le Prince de Beaumont's *Letters from Emerance to Lucy*.
54. *The Peruvian Letters. Translated from the French* (London, 1774), I, iv.
55. The concept of translation had, in fact, altered considerably by the end
of the century, as John Draper shows in "The Theory of Translation in the
Eighteenth Century," *Neophilologus*, VI (1912), 241–254. The critique, published in the *Analytical Review*, XII (April 1792), of Alexander Tytler, Lord
Woodhouselee's book *Essay on the Principles of Translation* indicates the standards acceptable by the last decade. A good translation was one "in which the
merit of the original work is so completely transfused into another language, as
to be distinctly apprehended, and as strongly felt, by a native of the country
to which that language belongs, as it is by those who speak the language of the
original work" (p. 413). Not denying the translator's right to "superadd" and
to eliminate "accessory" and "redundant" ideas, the critic believed that the

situations as unbelievable and coincidences as bizarre as anything in the untranslated sentimental fiction were presented without any effort to render them more probable. Nor did they alter characterization; an occasional footnote might chide exaggerated sentiments, but motives and emotions were left intact. They even respected, in most cases, the style and tone of language, adhering even to the sometimes extravagant punctuation.[56] England's view of continental sentimentality was, certainly, not complete; the translators' selection of available material served as a kind of initial censorship, protecting the readers from many extravagant displays of sensibility. Nevertheless, what the monolingual English public actually read in magazines and separate volumes was in most cases a faithful recreation of the sentimental fiction in vogue across the channel.

If the suppositions of publishers and translators concerning French sentimental fiction were correct—if they had accurately gauged the interest of the reading public in such a commodity and the literary conditions which might favor its acceptance—then the translations should have proved a successful commercial venture.

translation should not only "give a complete transcript of the ideas of the original work," but also that "the style and manner of writing should be of the same character with that of the original" (p. 415). "The duty of a translator," he concluded, "is not to improve upon his author, but to represent him faithfully" (p. 418). These standards were certainly observed in the majority of the French sentimental translations.

56. Two comparisons between the French and the English of translators who claimed to have been particularly scrupulous may be of interest. In Mme de Genlis' *Les Veillées du château* (Paris, 1819), a French noblewoman who has been rescued by two benevolent strangers exclaims, "après avoir vu tant d'ingrats, je goûte donc le plaisir de découvrir deux coeurs véritablement sensibles et reconnoissans!" (I, 117). Holcroft's noblewoman in *Tales of the Castle* says, "And have I at last, after meeting so much ingratitude in the world, have I at last the exquisite delight of finding two hearts truly sensible, truly noble!" (I, 96). Percival Stockdale's Lord Rivers writes to his ward, "But alas! You have lost that gentle, and affable Nature; that enchanting Sensibility which gave such animation, such irresistible Graces to your personal charm!" (I, 165). Mme Riccoboni's hero had asked simply, "Comment avez-vous perdu cette douceur, cette sensibilité qui ajoutoient des grâces si touchantes à vos agréments personnels?"—*Lettres de Milord Rivers, Oeuvres complètes* (Paris: Bassompierre, 1781), p. 176.

And indeed they did, as two facts demonstrate. Statistics on publication of translated French fiction, both in book and serialized form, show a pattern of initial acceptance in the sixties and seventies, a real enthusiasm from the mid-1770's to the mid-1790's, and the beginning of a decline in interest to 1800. And the reputation of those involved—publishing firms, magazines, and translators alike—indicates that the translated fiction was considered an honorable enterprise with which to be associated.

Of statistics concerning the two principal methods of dissemination of translations—novels issued by booksellers and stories printed in the periodicals—the first are more significant. In the first place, more original fiction was translated for the publishers, who were willing to pay. In the second, booksellers, unhindered by considerations of time and space, could turn out one, two, three, or more volumes and thus provide works of significance in their entirety to the public. In the third, it would appear that the publishers were rather sanguine about the mutability of novel readers' taste and, having successfully cultivated an interest in translated sentimental fiction, were unwilling to relinquish an audience so favorably disposed.

An analysis of the number of original translations of French sentimental fiction issued by the booksellers from 1760 to 1800 thus shows an interesting pattern.[57] The decade of the sixties marks the beginning of a noticeable increase in translated fiction. Whereas in the ten previous years, only sixteen novels (of all varieties) had been offered, from 1760–69 twenty-one specifically belonging to the sentimental genre appeared, fourteen of them in the last five years. That interest continued to develop steadily is proved by the growing number of original translations during each following

57. One complication in establishing any specific pattern, as Miss Tompkins points out, is that "the output of novels . . . slackens unaccountably in the half dozen years at the end of the 'seventies and the beginning of the 'eighties" (p. 13); translations from the French show the same diminution. In the following statistics I am including as "original" any new and different translation of an already-translated work. I have omitted anthologies; but one appeared in 1762, two in the seventies, seven in the eighties, and none in the nineties.

decade: twenty-three from 1770–79; a jump to thirty-four during
the 1780's; and, perhaps still more remarkable, a total of forty-
six from 1790 to 1800. When one adds to the original translations
the reprints and reeditions of previous works, the statistics become
still more impressive: twenty-nine from 1760–69; thirty-two from
1770–79; fifty-nine from 1780–89; and eighty-nine from 1790–
1800.

The magazines were simultaneously capitalizing on the interest
in sentimental translations from the French. An examination of the
number of stories published, reprinted, and borrowed—in other
words, the total number of appearances—each ten years shows,
like the statistics on the novels, that their popularity with the English was continually on the rise until the mid-nineties: forty-three
in the 1760's; fifty-five in the 1770's; eighty-nine in the 1780's;
and eighty-four in the 1790's. The total of 271 appearances repre-
sents over one quarter of the serialized fiction featured in the periodicals during those decades. Editors of the journals were apparently less confident about the appeal of translated fiction during the
last decade, however; for whereas booksellers continued to produce translations, foreign fiction disappeared almost completely
from the magazines after 1795.[58]

Any notion that the translations were considered merely ephem-
era and not worth the time of substantial booksellers is dispelled
by the names of the reputable firms who supplied the demand until William Lane's Minerva Press invaded the market during the
nineties.[59] The chief publishing house during the 1760's, for instance, was Becket and De Hondt; in addition to importing French

58. Only one new periodical translation appeared from 1795 to 1800, compared to twenty-six in the previous five years; and out of a total of eighty-four
appearances in the decade, only six occurred in the last half. I am, of course,
indebted to Mayo for statistics concerning periodical publication, as well as information given hereafter about the reputation of various journals.

59. Details about various publishing firms have been gathered largely from
H. R. Plomer, G. H. Bushnell, and E. R. McC. Dix, *A Dictionary of the Printers
and Booksellers Who Were at Work in England, Scotland, and Ireland from
1726 to 1775* (Oxford: Oxford University Press, 1932), and from John Nichols'
Literary Anecdotes.

literature and publishing periodical lists of new books from France, they issued fifteen new translations and were responsible for the English appearances of Rousseau's *Eloisa*, Marmontel's *Tales*, and five of Mme Riccoboni's novels. During the 1770's Becket and De Hondt furnished four translations; the same number was contributed by Cadell, the publisher of Johnson's *Lives of the Poets*, Gibbon's *Decline and Fall*, and Blackstone's *Commentaries*. Robinson, perhaps the most respected bookseller of his day, provided the largest number of translations in the 1780's, due principally to the efforts of Thomas Holcroft; hard on Robinson's heels were Hookham, who had four London stores through which he could dispose of his productions, and William Lane. By the 1790's the market unquestionably belonged to the latter's newly-named Minerva Press, which specialized in fiction for the circulating libraries.[60] During the last decade Lane issued thirteen translations, his closest competitors being Bew, a dealer in popular and ephemeral literature, with six and Vernor and Hood with five. Clearly, established firms as well as those with an eye to profit rather than quality nourished the vogue for sentimental fiction.

Certainly, frivolous or ephemeral periodicals contributed to the popularity of translated French fiction, but reputable, long-lived journals did their share, too. Most important was probably the *Lady's Magazine*, because of its particular interest in fiction and its subscription list of 10,000; it offered forty-two translated works to an eager feminine public. Second to the *Lady's* was the *Universal Magazine of Knowledge and Pleasure*, which directed itself to "Gentry, Merchants, Farmers, and Tradesmen"; and the foreign authors of the twenty-nine translations published therein shared the excellent British company of Fanny Burney, Mrs. Inchbald, Henry Brooke, and Charlotte Lennox. No other magazines matched these two in the quantity and quality of translations, although many others—especially provincial publications like the

60. Dorothy Blakey's comprehensive study *The Minerva Press, 1790–1820* (Oxford: Bibliographical Society at the University Press, 1939) furnishes both a history of Lane's firm and a bibliography of its publications.

Hibernian Magazine, the *Weekly Miscellany* of Glasgow, and Edinburgh's *Bee*—were busily printing and reprinting fiction for their public. Indeed, almost every English periodical, even the staid *Gentleman's Magazine*, included a few foreign stories during its lifetime; and journals like the *Critical Review* and the *Monthly Review* which made a practice of including long quotations as part of their critiques may equally be regarded as purveyors of French sentimental fiction.

The names of many of the translators, though unfamiliar today, were well known in their own time. Almost every prominent female writer, with the exception of Fanny Burney, tried her hand at translation, often as she was pursuing her own work independently. Typical was Elizabeth Griffith, who, after some translations of French nonfiction, set her own name for the first time to Dubois-Fontanelle's *Shipwreck and Adventures of Monsieur Pierre Viaud* (1771) and was known to be the translator of Dorat's *Fatal Effects of Inconstancy* (1774); meanwhile, she was turning out her own novels, *Delicate Distress* (1769), *The History of Lady Barton* (1771), and *The History of Lady Juliana Harley* (1776), works which earned the approbation of Clara Reeve as "moral and sentimental, [and] though they do not rise to the first class of excellence, they may fairly be ranked in the second" (II, 45). Other authoresses who followed the same pattern include Dr. Johnson's esteemed protegée Charlotte Lennox, author of *The Female Quixote* (1752) and translator of the *Count de Comminge* (1760); Frances Brooke, who signed her own *History of Lady Julia Mandeville* (1763) "By the translator of Lady Catesby's letters," her version of Mme Riccoboni's novel; Charlotte Smith, who, beginning her literary career with an illfated translation of Prévost's *Manon Lescaut* (1785), condensed Gayot de Pitaval's multi-volume *Causes célèbres* into the successful *Romance of Real Life* (1787) before producing original works like *Emmeline, or the Orphan of the Castle* (1788) and *Ethelinde, or the Recluse of the Lake* (1789); Clara Reeve, who identified *The Exiles* (1788), loosely based on D'Arnaud's "D'Almanzi," as by the "author of *The Old English*

Baron, Two Mentors, etc."; and Sophia Lee, whose *Warbeck: a Pathetic Tale* (1786) from D'Arnaud was "translated from the original French by the author of *The Recess*."

Other female translators, although more obscure than those previously mentioned, had some reputation among their contemporaries. After a highly publicized separation from her libertine husband, Susannah Gunning, née Minifie, wrote and signed five novels between 1790 and 1800, among them an English version of an anonymous work, *Love at First Sight* (1797); her daughter produced four identified works before 1800, of which two were translations from the French. One translation of St.-Pierre's *Paul et Virginie* was due to Helen Maria Williams, whose various *Letters* had communicated to her countrymen her ardent sympathy with the French during the early stages of the French Revolution. Mrs. Mary Pilkington's *Marmontel's Tales, Selected and abridged, for the Instruction and Amusement of Youth* (1799) was one of the earliest of the forty works that the moralizing authoress wrote between 1797 and 1825.

Fewer notable names are found among the gentlemen translators. Perhaps the most prominent was Thomas Holcroft, who, during a career as playwright, novelist, poet, and pamphleteer, managed also to translate fiction by Mme de Genlis, Mme de Montolieu, and Billardon de Sauvigny. William Shakespeare Kenrick was, in the words of Dr. Johnson, "one of the many who have made themselves *publick*, without making themselves *known*"; nevertheless, in addition to his duties as critic for the *Monthly Review* and editor of the *London Review of English and Foreign Literature*, he was the principal translator and defender of Rousseau. A frequenter of the Johnson circle, Percival Stockdale tried his hand at poetry, drama, and literary criticism—as well as Mme Riccoboni's *Letters from Lord Rivers* (1778)—with much production but little success. The benevolent translator of St.-Pierre, Edward Augustus Kendall, interspersed his literary activities with projects for founding colonies for distressed Indian halfcastes and West Indian mulattos. Daniel Malthus, who also translated *Paul et Virginie*, dabbled anonymously in literature and was the friend and executor of Rousseau, as well as the father of Thomas.

From a purely commercial standpoint, translators and publishers of the late eighteenth century may be complimented on their sagacity in anticipating a new literary market, supplying it with eminently suitable productions while interest continued, and retreating gracefully as demand called for newer fare. That translated French fiction had a certain degree of influence on indigenous British literature—suggesting to writers subjects and a particular tone and style appropriate to treating them—is undoubted.[61] Of equal interest, however, is its success as a competitor for public favor in a steadily-growing literature-oriented milieu. Who and what those British readers acclaimed is the final chapter in the history of the vogue of French sentimental fiction in late eighteenth-century England.

61. For a detailed examination of the influence of particular French novelists on eighteenth-century British writers, see James R. Foster's thorough study, *History of the Pre-Romantic Novel in English* (New York: Modern Language Association, 1949). J. M. S. Tompkins also notes points of contact between individual writers (Mme Riccoboni and Frances Brooke, D'Arnaud and Sophia Lee), common themes (inhumane confinement in prison or convent, penitence), and what she calls the "discouraging view" in both literatures that "broad humour and open passion are alike antiquated, and the modern reader must draw his amusement from the delicacies and ironies of sentiment" (p. 113).

CHAPTER THREE. PUBLIC ACCEPTANCE

To the booksellers and the translators must go considerable credit for anticipating and developing the vogue of translated French sentimental fiction; the statistics on publication prove their perspicacity. But this vogue testifies to more than commercial acumen: it is a reflection of that group which truly created and maintained it, the late eighteenth-century British reading public. What elements did this body of literature possess which made it attractive and congenial to the English? As a generalized portrait of the translated sentimental fiction will show, it was a genre whose very lack of national character made it extremely accessible to a foreign audience and whose content and subject matter could in general be applauded by even the most moral and traditional reader—provided he be, of course, a reader of sensibility. And what does its popularity say about its readers? It proves that in their literary preferences for sentimental authors—and here figures on publication, as well as English critics, will be called upon to bear witness —they were more like the French than they knew or, perhaps, might have cared to admit.

In considering French sentimental fiction as a genre, one cannot help but be struck by one element: its themes were deliberately universal, utilitarian, and conservative. It intended to teach man to behave more justly and humanely toward his fellows; and it did so not by appealing to any national code of ethics or values but by promoting that justice and virtue which spring instinctively from sensibility.[1] Thus, French sentimental fiction was, by its very pre-

1. Sensibility receives many accolades from the characters in sentimental fiction. The Count de B*** in Duclos' *The Pleasures of Retirement* (London, 1774) speaks of "a sentiment more penetrating than reason, nay even than wisdom herself . . . a sagacity of the heart, which is the measure of our sensibility" (I, 252). "Ah! the rare present that heaven makes us," says the father in Marmontel's "The Samnite Marriages," *Moral Tales* (London, 1764), "when he gives us a sensible heart! It is the principle of all the virtues" (II, 63). Dolerval, the hero of Louvet de Couvrai's *Emily de Varmont* (London, 1798),

mises, supra-national in emphasis. Sensibility was a common de-
nominator on both sides of the channel; and the human heart, free
of social or moral prejudice, was to be the source of right and
proper action.[2] At the same time, however, it believed that reason
would hold to traditional and conservative institutions as long as
they corresponded to the natural order and to the promptings of
sensibility.

One universal doctrine preached continually by sentimental fiction was the rightness and the necessity of religious feeling. Religion was the natural product of the spirit of man who, in
encountering the world around him, deduced by both instinct and
reason the existence of a supreme being.[3] His vision of God was
that of a merciful and understanding master who realized the
frailties of His mortal creations; therefore, religion compassion-

---

delivers an impassioned declaration of its merits: "You laugh at my sensibility!
but are you ignorant that to it I am indebted for the most refined pleasures that
I ever enjoy? . . . without it, my heart would perhaps not melt to pity in the
cottage of misery and distress" (II, 117).

2. The sentimental novelists did, of course, acknowledge that sensibility, in
order to manifest itself justly, should be properly restrained. The principal
theme of many of the novels is, in fact, as Mme de Genlis declares in the ded-
ication to *Rash Vows* (London, 1799), to show "the dangerous consequences
of excessive delicacy and extreme sensibility . . . [and that] without wisdom,
and consequently without moderation, sensibility is only a fatal gift" (I, iii–iv).
Other novels which lecture on the dangers of sensibility include Ducray–Dumi-
nil's *Alexis, or the Cottage in the Woods* (which the author in the untranslated
preface claims to be a satire on sensibility), Mme de Charrière's *Letters Written
from Lausanne*, Dubois-Fontanelle's *The Effects of the Passions*, Dorat's *The
Fatal Effects of Inconstancy*, and "The History of M. de la Paliniere" in Mme
de Genlis' *Tales of the Castle*.

3. In Mme Le Prince de Beaumont's *The Triumph of Truth*, for example,
the atheist M. de la Vilette compacts with his devout wife to bring up their
child without religious instruction and finds himself convinced of the necessity
of an all-governing will by his twelve-year-old's reasoning. Beaurieu's hero in
The Man of Nature (London, 1773) similarly deduces a divinity from the in-
tricate reciprocal relationships which he observes between animals and nature.
"It must be then, that this Supreme Will is a Being, infinitely powerful, infinitely wise—O great and omnipotent Being, the sun, myself, and all that exist,
exist by thee alone! I acknowledge thy powers, thy wisdom, thy goodness: I
thank thee, I adore thee!" (I, 247–248).

ately and indulgently comforted the erring and afflicted.[4] Need-less to say, only Christianity (nonsectarian, it should be added) embodied these qualities; sentiment did not encourage cultist experimentation, let alone heresy.[5]

After love of God, sentimental literature promoted love of family. The duties of wife towards husband, father towards child, and child towards parent were inevitably fulfilled if each behaved as his heart commanded.[6] Inevitably, each did not; fiction demands conflicts, and conjugal waywardness, filial disobedience, or parental abuse frequently supplied them.[7] But family reconciliations, accompanied by the maximum display of repentant tears and joy,

4. Marmontel, in the controversial fifteenth chapter of *Belisarius* (London, 1767), insists on both points. "The triumph of religion," according to his hero, "is to administer consolation in the hour of adversity and to mingle in the cup of sorrow the sweets of calm delight" (p. 204) ; God must be a merciful being, since "From the hands of my Creator I came forth weak and feeble; he will be indulgent therefore; to him it is apparent that I have neither the madness nor the wickedness to offend him" (p. 207).

5. The heroine of Lavallée's *Maria Cecilia; or Life and Adventures of the Daughter of Achmet III, Emperor of the Turks* (London, 1788), is a convert to Christianity who ascribes her perseverance in adversity to the "astonishing courage we derive from the Christian religion" (I, 75) ; likewise comforted by Christianity are Zelida, the converted pagan in D'Arnaud's *The History of Count Gleichen*, and the cast-away heroine of Mme Daubenton's *Zelia in the Desert*.

6. Family affection is preached incessantly by Mme de Genlis in such works as *The Rival Mothers*, *Tales of the Castle*, and *Adelaide and Theodore*; by Marmontel in "The Error of a Good Father," "The School for Fathers," "The Good Mother," and "A Wife of Ten Thousand!"; and is also a prominent feature of Rousseau's *Eloisa*, Mme Daubenton's *Zelia in the Desert*, Mme de Charrière's *Letters Written from Lausanne*, and Mme D'Ormoy's "Amelia, a Novel."

7. In Marmontel's "The Good Husband," "The Sylph Husband," and "The Happy Divorce," the frivolous heroines are discontented with the conjugal state. Julia in D'Arnaud's "Julia or the Penitent Daughter," Rosetta in the same author's "The History of Rosetta," and Aspasia in Mme Benoît's *Aspasia; or the Dangers of Vanity* desert their families to seek excitement in the world. Cécile's father in Mme de Genlis' *Adelaide and Theodore* forces his daughter to take the veil, as does Lucile's in Marmontel's "The Two Unfortunate Ladies"; and in the latter's "Lausus and Lydia" the tyrannical father is on the verge of putting his son to death for loving a charming but ineligible maiden.

provided happy endings and reaffirmed the reader's conviction in the rightfulness of domestic harmony.[8]

After love of God and family, sentimental literature inspired love of one's fellow man. This was no abstract concept. Metaphysical or ethical speculation was greatly disdained in these novels, and concrete, active philanthropy advocated with enthusiasm.[9] Benevolence might vary from the trivial to the grandiose—from a few pennies extended to a needy pauper to entire farms and villages rebuilt for starving peasants.[10] Charity was by no means, how-

8. A favorite scene in sentimental fiction is the reunion between parent and child, separated by either accident or misfortune. Notable examples occur in *The Man of Nature*, where the hero instinctively recognizes the father he has never seen; D'Auvigny's *Memoirs of Madame Barneveldt*; Mme Benoît's *Aspasia*; Mme de Genlis' "The History of the Duchess of C***," who is restored to her family after ten years of incarceration inflicted on her by a jealous husband; Lavallée's *Maria Cecilia*, where the daughter hastens from Turkey to rescue her father from a Parisian prison; and Gorjy's *Victorina*, in which not only the heroine but also her benefactress simultaneously rediscovers her long-lost parents.

9. A quotation from Florian's *The Adventures of Numa Pompilius, Second King of Rome* (London, 1787) well summarizes this point of view. "Can you imagine that heaven has endowed you with talents and virtues for yourself alone? Do you think to please God by living only for yourself?" demands a Roman of Numa; "The Supreme Being considers vain speculations as of no value; he requires an active virtue . . . and can only regard those with favour, who are industrious in promoting the happiness of mankind" (II, 190). There is, in fact, a profoundly anti-philosophical current in the translated fiction. Julia in D'Arnaud's story is corrupted by the "pernicious discourses" of "Freethinkers and Libertines"; Elise in Mme Le Prince de Beaumont's "The True Point of Honour," *Moral Tales* (London, 1775), attributes her cousin's escapades to "what they call philosophy. . . . Ah! unhappy victim of these corrupters of the public, how much do I pity you!"(I, 156). Similar sentiments are expressed in the latter's *The New Clarissa*, in St.-Pierre's *Paul and Virginia* and *The Indian Cottage*, and in Mme de Genlis' *Tales of the Castle*.

10. Among the more elaborate examples of active benevolence are the rural utopias described in Rousseau's *Eloisa* and Mme Le Prince de Beaumont's *The New Clarissa* and the ideal Christian society set up by Camira, Angélique, and the priest Maldonado among the Paraguyan natives in Florian's "Camira." Notably benevolent landlords include Sainville in Mme de Genlis' *Rash Vows*, Noirval and St. Ange in Constant de Rebècque's *Laura, or Letters from Switzerland*, Therese's father's friend in Léonard's *The Correspondence of Two Lovers*, Emilia in Mme de Souza's *Emilia and Alphonsus*, the Count in Marmontel's "The Scruple," and Arsaces in Montesquieu's "Arsaces and Ismenia."

ever, egalitarian in sentimental literature. Although it showed a genuine concern for the alleviation of the most extreme social evils, it aimed at maintaining the social status quo. Peasants profited from their masters' goodwill, but they were not encouraged to replace them.[11] Nor did sentimental literature preach a disinterested benevolence. Always associated with active philanthropy was an intense personal satisfaction at the sight of those persons whose condition one had helped to improve; and emotional scenes of gratitude were often used to excite similarly benevolent feelings in the bosom of the reader.[12]

Sentimental literature did not neglect lessons on the good life and how to live it. Simplicity and moderation were proper and natural, overly-civilized luxury generally to be avoided.[13] These

11. Rousseau is perhaps the least equivocal about the matter. In *Eloisa* (London, 1784) Julia says to St.-Preux, "we do not converse with peasants, indeed, in the style of the courts; but we treat them with a grave and distant familiarity which, without raising any one out of his station, teaches them to respect our's" (III, 233). And her old friend summarizes "Mrs. Wolmar's great maxim [which] is never to encourage any one to change his condition, but to contribute all in her power to make everyone happy in his present station" (III, 234).

12. "The pleasure of conferring happiness is so sweet, so alluring, that the heart which has once tasted it can never renounce the gratification. It affords to such a person the most sublime delight" (I, 115), asserts the Countess in Mme Le Prince de Beaumont's "The True Point of Honour." Typical of an emotional scene of gratitude is that in Carra's *Cecilia: or the Eastern Lovers* (London, 1773): " 'May you live! live long! for you are worthy of it!' " cries an old man to his benefactor, while "At the same time the tears gushed from his eyes and streamed down his reverend cheeks, as from an inexhaustible source of pleasure; thus was I a second time paid for my bounty, with uxorious interest" (pp. 45–46). Other notable instances of gratitude include the "respect and obedience" of a grateful band of "ferocious savages" when the hero of Mme de Genlis' "The Slaves; or, the Benefit Repaid," *Tales of the Castle*, buys and reunites a black child with his mother; the anniversary celebration instituted by a village to commemorate the hero's saving the population from the Moors in Florian's "Pedro and Celestina"; and in D'Arnaud's *Sidney and Volsan* the Temple of Gratitude which the latter erects to the former and in which he and his family worship each day.

13. The "primitive" societies—that is, those at the greatest distance from European influence—display the most natural and laudable organization: Marmontel's Incas and the family group in St.-Pierre's *Paul and Virginia*. An individual from such a society is invariably superior to civilized man and instructs him in honor and sentiment, like Zilia in Mme de Graffigny's *The*

precepts provided another source of conflict necessary to the fiction. Perpetual dichotomies were set up: between the city, which depraves and corrupts, and the country, which calms and mends; between the peasant or farmer, who labors in accord with nature, and the noble, who exists by the toil or the ruin of others.[14] Those countryfolk were often, it is true, aristocrats or bourgeois who had retreated to the country because of straitened circumstances; but they invariably lived more justly and more righteously than their city counterparts.[15]

Peruvian Letters, Coraly in Marmontel's "Friendship Put to the Test," the pariah in St.-Pierre's *The Indian Cottage*, and Itanoko in Lavallée's *The Negro Equalled by Few Europeans*. Closer to home and therefore a more familiar figure in sentimental literature is, of course, the peasant, a virtuous primitive in his own right since, as St.-Preux says in *Eloisa*, "Neither their hearts nor understandings are formed by art; they have not learned to model themselves after the fashion, and are less the creatures of men than those of nature" (III, 264).

14. Many a virtuous heroine is ruined when she leaves the country for the city—the central lesson of Marmontel's "Lauretta" and D'Arnaud's "Julia" and "The History of Rosetta"; and many a hero is temporarily diverted from dissipation by a sojourn in the country, as in D'Arnaud's *Fanny, or the Happy Repentance* and *The Exiles* and Duclos' *The Confessions of the Count de B****. Moreover, when there is a villain in sentimental literature, he is inevitably a worldly-wise, coldly rational, city-dwelling aristocrat: Sir Thomas Ward in *Fanny*; Valville in Mme Elie de Beaumont's *The History of the Marquis de Roselle*; the Duke in Dorat's *The Fatal Effects of Inconstancy*; the Comte d'Olban (who eventually redeems himself) in Mme D'Ormoy's "Amelia"; and Lormon, who patterns himself on Lovelace, in Imbert's "Rosetta."

15. Rank is treated somewhat ambivalently in sentimental fiction; but providing parents or spouses who, in spite of their country residence, are in fact gentlefolk upholds in a subtle manner a conservative attitude toward birth. The novel heroine who marries an apparently lower-class husband has not, it generally happens, done anything degrading: the heroine of *The New Clarissa* runs away with an undistinguished young man to escape from her angry father and marries him to preserve her virtuous reputation, after which it is revealed that her husband is an impoverished baron; Sara Th—— in St.-Lambert's "The History of Sara Th——," *Original Tales, Histories, Essays and Translations* (Edinburgh, 1785), marries out of esteem and shows "a proper degree of respect for salutary prejudices" (p. 32) by living in the country, but her husband is actually the son of a Scottish noble stripped of his title for having supported the Jacobite rebellion. D'Arnaud's Fanny and Julia, who marry aristocrats, are the daughters of gentlemen—the former, even, of an Oxford graduate.

In sentimental literature, individual rights and freedoms, when pursued according to the dictates of nature and sensibility, were generally opposed to artificial social conventions and prejudices.[16] This principle often led to situations which out of context might have seemed immoral or aberrant: marriage unsanctified by the church; illegitimacy; bigamy; even incest.[17] But the reader was expected to understand and sympathize with—if not to emulate— the erring characters. Provided that in straying beyond the bounds of society's conventions, they remained within the bounds of nature's, their sensibility, always alive to natural impulse, guaranteed them an innocent purity and therefore the right to the reader's respect and esteem.[18]

16. "Let us no longer hesitate to forsake a world whose very laws are an encouragement to vice," Mirbelle urges Mme de Syrcé in Dorat's *Fatal Effects of Inconstancy*, 2nd ed. (London, 1777), "where the phantom Honour, upon a thousand cruelties and wrongs, erects its throne, levying rebellious war against the empire of Nature. Hers is the standard of her subjects. Hers are the laws of her creatures" (II, 186–187). This is, of course, the most customary justification of illicit love affairs, since marriage is frequently presented as nothing more than a social or economic arrangement between two otherwise incompatible people.

17. Over and beyond the question of illicit affairs, marriage in the eyes of God and nature—if not of the church—is often claimed to excuse sincere and tender lovers; it appears in *Zelia in the Desert*, in *The Man of Nature*, in *Cecilia: or the Eastern Lovers*, in Mme Riccoboni's *The History of Christine of Swabia*, and in Marmontel's "Anette and Lubin" and "The Shepherdess of the Alps," the most popular of all his stories. An illegitimate child, the pardonable fruit of passion, is a feature of *Zelia*, Loaisel de Tréogate's *Julius or the Natural Son*, Florian's "Claudine," Mlle Fauques' "The Triumph of Friendship," Gorjy's *Blansay*, and Mme de Genlis' *Rival Mothers*, whose hero has not one but two bastards. Bigamy is the theme of D'Arnaud's *The History of Count Gleichen*, and incest occurs in *Julius*.

18. Heroines who go astray are often treated more kindly, thus, than strict morality might prescribe, and any of them might merit Dorat's tribute to Mme de Syrcé: "The foibles of a well disposed mind bring on misfortune, give offence to prejudices, but do not always annihilate virtue . . . [and] the woman who yields is often more courageous than she who resists" (I, iii). A similar comment is made in Mme Daubenton's *Zelia* (London, 1789) to the unwedded but pregnant Nina: "Restore to yourself, my dear friend, that esteem which no mortal would refuse you, did they know, as I do, the purity of your heart" (I, 72). And even when an erring heroine does die, thereby appeasing propriety, she expires only after one or more volumes have been expended on

Just as the basic assumptions made by French sentimental fiction concerning behavior and psychology went beyond any national character to some sort of universal generalizations about human virtue and morality, so too were its settings, chronology, and characters international in scope. Because it was neither satiric in intent nor particularly realistic in presentation, it wasted little time on analysis of specific milieux. Rather, it chose any historical period and any exotic locale that seemed to offer an appropriate setting for its moral preoccupations. Stories took place in various European countries, in the Near East, and in South America; they might be set in some vague classical epoch, in the never-never land of pastoralism, or in a definite but vaguely described medieval period.[19] Characters were by no means exclusively French; foreigners of every race and description peopled the fiction. If one foreign nation might be especially singled out in the translated stories, it was in fact the English—a circumstance that could scarcely have displeased the British readers, since their countrymen were always represented with the greatest respect, their history portrayed in glorious and brave colors, and their homeland described in admiring terms.[20]

---

her struggles: Camille in Mme de Genlis' *Rival Mothers* and Henrietta in Framéry's *The Memoirs of the Marquis de St. Forlaix* suffer through four volumes; Constance dies in the third volume of Mme de Genlis' *Rash Vows*; and the Marchioness de Syrcé and Caliste in *Letters Written from Lausanne* perish after one volume of tribulation.

19. To cite as examples only the works of Florian: his *New Tales* are set in Africa, Savoy, India, South America, and Italy, and the three of his *Six Nouvelles* translated into English take place in Persia, Spain, and Greece; *Numa Pompilius* is a novel of Rome during the time of Romulus; *Estelle* is a pastoral; and *Gonsalvo of Cordova* describes the Moors' assault on Spain in the Middle Ages.

20. Enlightened Englishmen and Englishwomen are prominent, for example, in *Eloisa*, *The New Clarissa*, "Sara Th——," Mme Riccoboni's *Letters from Lord Rivers*, *The History of Jenny Salisbury*, and *Letters from Juliet Lady Catesby*, Mme de Genlis' *Rash Vows*, Dorat's *The Fatal Effects of Inconstancy*, Dubois-Fontanelle's *Shipwreck and Adventures of Pierre Viaud*, and St.-Pierre's *The Indian Cottage*. The fiction of D'Arnaud is particularly interesting in this respect. Out of sixteen novels and stories translated, English characters and settings figure in eight; in two cases, *Sidney and Volsan* and

Broadly stated, thus, these French sentimental novels and stories were as a body accessible and congenial to a British reader because of the universality of their precepts and the absence of a too-national literary character in subject matter and treatment. As they had pleased the French audience for whom they were written, so they pleased the British public for whom they were translated—a fact which suggests that literary taste, in this instance at least, was much the same on both sides of the channel. There is, indeed, further evidence for this contention. If one examines those authors most popular with the English public, both in magazine and in book form, and if one compares the comments made by both English and French critics concerning them, one becomes aware of a similarity of judgment not simply the product of chance but of genuinely congruent opinion.

When Rousseau's *Julie ou la nouvelle Héloïse* appeared in France in 1761, it won immediate popularity with the public; but seldom had a novel provoked such divided critical opinion. The story was immoral, said many. Julie was immodest and presumptuous; St.-Preux was too resigned a lover, Wolmar too complaisant a husband; the passion described in the first part was cheapened by the domestic arrangements in the following. Eleven years later the abbé Chaudon would still protest that "la fiction, l'exposition, le noeud, le dénouement ne sont pas à l'abri d'une juste censure."[21] On the other hand, the expressive emotion found favor with all. "L'éloquence du coeur, le ton du sentiment, cette douce mélancholie qui n'est connue que dans la retraite, un goût exquis de la Nature physique et moral, un génie mâle et fléxible qui sçait la contempler

---

"The Rival Friends," an Englishman plays the magnanimous benefactor to the unfortunate foreigner. "The New Clementina" is admittedly modelled on Richardson and justified by D'Arnaud's effusive opinion concerning "The Character of Richardson" which the *Universal* included in the same issue. That the French sentimental authors admired, and deliberately used, the British in their fiction is undoubted; that English translators capitalized on their admiration when they chose works to present should not be unexpected.

21. Louis-Mayeul Chaudon, *Bibliothèque d'un homme de goût, ou avis sur les choix des meilleurs livres écrits en notre langue sur tous les genres de sciences et de littérature* (Avignon, 1772), II, 256.

dans sa grandeur et la saisir dans ses détails" was what the *Année Littéraire* "ne peut refuser à M. Rousseau."[22] Praise and admiration eventually triumphed. "Malheur à celui qui ne sentirait que les défauts!" cried Palissot; "Malheur à celui que les beautés de détails, dont abonde ce charmant Ouvrage, ne transportent et n'affectent pas délicieusement, et qui ne s'attendrit pas pour les vertus dans les admirables peintures que l'Auteur en a sçu tracer!"[23]

In England *La Nouvelle Héloïse* was greeted with immediate attention; and even before William Kenrick translated it, the French original had been reviewed by the three major critical periodicals of the time.[24] The *Gentleman's Magazine*—perhaps the most respected of the journals, the one not given to noticing trifles and the one most addicted to generalized clichés—found that the work's subjects were "treated in a masterly manner, and the story which is simple is conducted with an air of truth and nature that is seldom to be met with in this kind of writting [sic]."[25] Comparing him to Richardson, the *Monthly Review* felt that Rousseau "seems not only to have happily imitated his manner, but to have excelled in purity of style."[26] The *Critical Review*, a little concerned about the Frenchman's previous philosophical speculations, decided that in the novel, "he, in some measure, lays the philosopher aside, and mixes in the chearful ways of men, paints with the most luxuriant

22. *L'Année Littéraire*, ed. Elie Fréron (1761), II, 313–314, hereafter cited as *AL*.

23. *Les Mémoires pour servir à l'histoire de notre littérature, depuis François I jusqu'à nos jours*, Vol. IV in *Oeuvres complettes de M. Palissot* (Liège et Paris, 1778), 331.

24. James Warner has studied "Eighteenth-Century English Reactions to the *Nouvelle Heloise*" in detail in *PMLA*, LII (September 1937), 803–819; see also his useful listings of editions in "A Bibliography of Eighteenth-Century English Editions of J. J. Rousseau, with Notes on the Early Diffusion of his Writings," *PQ*, XIII (July 1934), 225–247, and the supplement, "Addenda to the Bibliography of Eighteenth-Century Editions of J. J. Rousseau," *PQ*, XIX (July 1940), 237–243.

25. *Gentleman's Magazine*, XXXI (January 1761), 34, hereafter cited as *Gentleman's*.

26. *Monthly Review or Literary Journal*, XXIII (December 1760), 492, hereafter cited as *Monthly*.

imagination, and interests every passion with the most bewitching art."[27]

Just as *La Nouvelle Héloïse* enjoyed enormous popularity with the French audience, the appearance of *Eloisa; or a Series of Original Letters*, as Kenrick called his translation, in 1761 was the beginning of four decades of remarkable success with the English public. The *Monthly* and the *Critical* used their reviews of the translation as an excuse to publish several of the letters for the benefit of the public; the *London Magazine* did its own five-part translation of material it considered most instructive. Between 1761 and 1795, *Eloisa* went through ten editions. The novel, in the *Critical*'s opinion, was not equal but superior to Richardson's *Clarissa*. To the "exquisitely delicate" Clarissa, "prudent, perhaps, to a degree of coldness," the reviewer opposed Julia, "full of sensibility," who swerves from the path of virtue but is "reclaimed by the horror of her crime, and her innate purity of sentiment." He found Rousseau's work "infinitely more sentimental, animated, refined, and elegant," for the French author "lays naked the heart at a single stroke."[28]

The slightly dubious morality of the novel which the French critics had perceived when it appeared did not begin to trouble the English until somewhat later in the century. In a review of a spurious sequel to *Eloisa* called *Letters of an Italian Nun and an English Gentleman* (1781), the *Gentleman's* commented that "the licentiousness of John James is indeed too apparent; but where is the art, the delicacy, the sensibility with which he instills his poison, and which makes us admire even while we detest him?"[29] Writing in *The Progress of Romance*, Clara Reeve was concerned about the novel's portrayal of passion: "It is a book that speaks to the heart, and engages that in its behalf, and when reflexion comes afterwards, and reason takes up the reins, we discover that it is

27. *Critical Review; or, Annals of Literature*, XI (January 1761), 65, hereafter cited as *Critical*.
28. *Critical*, XII (September 1761), 204-205.
29. *Gentleman's*, LIII (January 1783), 55.

dangerous and improper for those for whose use it is chiefly intended, for young persons." She was in the long run indulgent, however; if Rousseau had meant to exhibit the evils of gallantry, "he is to be commended; and if it produced effects he did not foresee, he ought to be excused."[30] As late as 1798, a critic for the *Analytical Review* would still choose to make his point about a current production by asserting that "the simplest narrative, as in the incomparable *Héloïse* of Rousseau, may be rendered exquisitely interesting, [when] embellished by the graces of sentiment and expression."[31]

It may be instructive to point out how the *Eloisa*, surely the most distinguished of the French sentimental novels, conforms to the generalizations set forth at the beginning of this chapter. The setting is Switzerland, a country whose aspects, alternately wild and tranquil, evoked the descriptions of nature which formed an essential part of the book's charm. The time is not precisely contemporary, for the action begins in the mid-1730's. As to the characters, Julie and St.-Preux are Swiss, Wolmar a Russian, and the benevolent and enlightened Lord Bomston an Englishman. Except for St.-Preux's critical and satirical letters from Paris, the focus of attention is the country and the simple and easy pleasures to be found there. All of the moral lessons typical of sentimental fiction as a genre appear, embodied in Julie: her sincere piety (which eventually converts her atheist husband), her tender maternal affection, the active benevolence which she practices as mistress of Clarens. And they demonstrate to the reader that Julie's trusting dependence on heart and sensibility as guides to virtue does indeed

30. *The Progress of Romance* (1785; rpt New York: Facsimile Text Society, 1930), II, 13–14, hereafter cited in the text.

31. *Analytical Review; or, History of Literature, Domestic and Foreign,* XXVII (April 1798), 415, hereafter cited as *Analytical*. Rousseau's popularity with the English was such that he had the dubious honor of being credited—after his death—with several sequels to *Eloisa*: the previously-mentioned *Letters of an Italian Nun*, which had two editions in 1781 and a reprint in 1784; and *Laura; or Original Letters*, which actually came from the German of F. A. C. Werthes, translated via a French version, but which was appended to the 1784 and 1795 editions of *Eloisa* and separately published by Lane in 1790.

create a world of harmony and bliss. Nor did the utility of Julie's affair with St.-Preux, her dishonor and moral reinstatement, go unappreciated; as the *Critical Review* observed in 1761, it is a most "instructive lesson to the female world, who generally resign over to vice those of their own sex, who have once deviated from the paths of virtue, though earnest to redeem their errors."[32]

Although perhaps the most esteemed French author, Rousseau was not the most popular with the English reading public. That honor was reserved for Marmontel, whose entire output of fiction was continually translated and retranslated throughout the last four decades of the century. Publication in book form of his works testifies to their remarkable and consistent appeal for the British audience. Although a first, timid translation of his *contes*, called *Select Moral Tales*, had gone unnoticed in 1763, two complete English translations appeared simultaneously the next year: one, done by Charles Denis and Robert Lloyd, was published by Kearsley; the other, more favorably received by the critics, was presented anonymously by Becket and De Hondt and augmented by a third volume in 1766. Reissues of both of these versions during subsequent decades added up to seven editions before 1800.[33] In addition, Marmontel was judged suitable even for the children; Mrs. Mary Pilkington offered her translation of *Marmontel's Tales, Selected and Abridged, for the Instruction and Amusement of Youth* in 1799. *Belisarius* was likewise enthusiastically received: nine editions appeared between 1767 and 1800. Translations of *The Incas* and the *New Moral Tales* met with less success: the former had one edition in 1777, published in both England and Ireland, and another in 1797; the latter saw two editions and was the object of two different translations.

32. *Critical*, XII (September 1761), 205.

33. Paul Kaufman, in *Borrowings from the Bristol Library, 1773–1784: a Unique Record of Reading Vogues* (Charlottesville: Bibliographical Society of the University of Virginia, 1960), records that Marmontel's *Tales*, in the Denis and Lloyd translation, was taken out seventy-nine times during those years—a figure in the Belles Lettres section surpassed only by Johnson's *Lives of the Poets, Tristram Shandy*, and the works of Swift and Fielding.

Marmontel furnishes perhaps the most noteworthy—and the most interesting—example of the congruence of French and English sentimental taste during the latter part of the eighteenth century. First, general critical opinion of his talent, based principally on the *Contes moraux*, was almost identical on both sides of the channel. It found him occasionally witty and amusing but, all in all, discovered more to blame than to praise. The *Journal de Politique et de Littérature*, commenting on a new edition of the *Contes moraux* in 1776, reproached him for "Un style souvent affecté, qu'un Censeur austère pourroit appeller *jargon*, quelques situations intéressantes, peu d'imagination, et même de légérté, malgré les efforts de l'Auteur pour n'être pas pesant, plus de connoissances des manières du monde que du coeur humain, et plus de soin à s'approprier le persifflage, le papillotage de nos cercles, que de capacité pour la peinture des passions."[34] Twenty-two years earlier, the *Critical* had said of the *Moral Tales*, "we cannot but be of the opinion, that the dialogue, in many of them, is tedious, and the sentiments spun out in such a manner, as to make them pall upon the reader's appetite"[35]; and the *Monthly* had found his descriptions of character "too general—undistinguished by those fine discriminations of mind, those peculiar colourings of passion and sentiment, that vary, more or less, in every individual."[36]

And both French and English critics ascribed these shortcomings to precisely the same reason: Marmontel had deliberately adapted his style and subject matter to suit contemporary French taste. The *Journal de Politique* declared, "Le sort au moins momentané de ce Recueil est décidé: on ne le mettra probablement jamais au rang des Ouvrages qui illustrent un siècle: mais il pourra être apprécié par la posterité comme un de ceux qui caractérisent le nôtre."[37] Chaudon said of him, "Il a voulu écrire pour son

34. *Journal de Politique et de Littérature*, 25 Mars 1776, pp. 383–384.
35. *Critical*, XVII (January 1764), 44.
36. *Monthly*, XXX (January 1764), 59–60.
37. *Journal de Politique et de Littérature*, 25 Mars 1776, p. 383.

siècle, et il a réussi."[38] This tendency was rather atypical in a translated sentimental writer; and the English found it not a subject of admiration but one of reproach. The *Critical* attributed "the author's light airy manner . . . [to] the prevailing taste of his countrymen."[39] As late as 1792, the reviewer for the *Analytical* ascribed Marmontel's "Gallantry and the *prettiness* of sentiment" to his being forced to draw his characters from a people interested in "a kind of refined *gentlemanly* sensuality, that rendered their taste vicious, and ever at war with nature"; and "unable to rise above his native atmosphere, he has faithfully delineated some prevailing passions modified by the national character."[40]

Second, though critics might censure the stories, the remarkable frequency with which they appeared in the English periodicals of the day testifies to the favor they found with British readers.[41] Out of 130 stories which the magazines published in the 1760's, thirty-two were by the French writer—almost twenty percent of the total appearances of fiction in the decade. During the 1770's his stories appeared seventeen times and during the 1780's only nine; but

38. Louis-Mayeul Chaudon and Joseph Laporte, *Nouvelle Bibliothèque d'un homme de goût, ou tableau de la littérature ancienne et moderne, étrangère et nationale* (Paris, 1777), II, 262.

39. *Critical*, XX (December 1765), 449.

40. *Analytical*, XII (February 1792), 218–219. Opinions at home and abroad differed more widely on the merits of *Belisarius* and *The Incas*. The French were displeased by Marmontel's efforts to mix fiction and philosophy, for they felt in general that the former had been sacrificed to the latter. The English were profoundly impressed with both works because of the patriotic and benevolent sentiments they contained. According to the *Gentleman's*, *Belisarius* was filled with "incidents the most natural and tender, sentiments the most elegant and sublime, and principles of government in the highest degree just, generous and heroic": XXXVII (April 1767), 180. The *Monthly* felt that *The Incas* contained "such a variety of just and manly sentiments" that it must obtain "the warmest applause from every true lover of liberty and friend of mankind": LVIII (May 1778), 336.

41. Marmontel's stories appeared first, in fact, in the magazines. The very first to be translated was "Anette and Lubin," which timidly appeared without Marmontel's name in, oddly enough, the *Gentleman's*, September 1761; subsequently Denis and Lloyd translated several of them in 1763 for the latter's *St. James's Magazine* before they gathered them between hard covers.

New Moral Tales in 1792 signaled a revival of interest, and stories from that collection, as well as from the earlier one, were printed thirty-one times during the nineties. All in all, twenty-eight of Marmontel's *contes* appeared eighty-nine times from 1760 to 1800.[42] Nor were these appearances simply reprints of the anthologized translations. A number were new versions (the *Lady's Magazine* in particular encouraged original efforts in the early eighties); and "L'Amitié à l'épreuve," known variously as "The Trial of Friendship" and "Friendship Put to the Test," came out in at least three different translations on seven different occasions.[43] These statistics suggest very strongly that Marmontel's stories—which had, of course, been written specifically to enliven the *Mercure de France*—pleased and satisfied the British magazine-reading public in the same way that they had pleased and satisfied the same audience in France.

A brief digression about a minor author may serve to reinforce this idea of similarity of sentimental literary taste. Among the multitude of French authors who followed in Marmontel's footsteps and capitalized on the success of the new genre was Bricaire de la Dixmérie, whose *Contes moraux et philosophiques* (1765) were, according to the *Bibliothèque d'un homme de goût*, "les plus lus" and "écrits agréablement et avec l'aménité que le sujet demande."[44] They did not resemble Marmontel's by accident; La Dixmérie wrote them for the *Mercure* after Marmontel had left the journal. Interestingly enough, the *Contes* were never translated in book form in England; hence, La Dixmérie received no critical attention and no recognition from the public. The magazines pil-

42. It should be noted as well that Marmontel's name figured almost invariably in the titles of translations—a further indication that the English were well acquainted with his reputation and talent, as was the flattering series of imitations begun in 1774 by the *St. James's Magazine* called "The English Marmontel, or the School of Sentiment."

43. The most popular *conte*, however, was "La Bergère des Alpes," for in addition to seven periodical appearances, it was separately published five times.

44. Chaudon, II, 263.

laged the French collection, however: five translations appeared in the 1760's, seven in the 1770's, eight in the 1780's, and two in the 1790's. Nine stories were printed a total of twenty-two times; yet his name appeared on only two, and only six appearances were even identified as "From the French"—a notable example of the ease with which French sentimental stories were assimilated into contemporary magazine fiction.

"One of the most pathetic and moral writers now in France; and in many essentials of this species of composition might be compared to the immortal author of *Clarissa*": thus wrote the *European Magazine* of Baculard d'Arnaud, whose success with the English public was in a way as remarkable as that of Marmontel.[45] His fictional appearances—tentative during the 1760's, increasingly regular during the 1770's and 1780's—illustrate to some extent the pattern of the vogue of French sentimental fiction in Britain. A novel called *Fanny, or Injur'd Innocence* was published by Becket in 1766; the reviewers deprecated it, although the *Universal Magazine* excerpted it in July of that year. Nothing more by the French writer appeared until a booklength Dublin translation of "Sidney et Volsan" in 1772. The next year the *Universal* borrowed "The History of Rosetta" from John Murdoch's *Tears of Sensibility*, four translated stories extracted from D'Arnaud's *Epreuves du sentiment*; and interest was evidently keen enough by this point to encourage a series of translations from his voluminous *Epreuves* and *Nouvelles historiques*. Something brand-new by him, either a serialized story or a separately-published novel, appeared nearly every year from 1773 to 1788. And although no English translation of any major story from his multi-volume *Délassemens de l'homme sensible* was ever done, the *Monthly* and the *European* both took the time to review and to praise the foreign work.[46] All in all, fourteen of his

45. *European Magazine and London Review*, IV (December 1783), 450, hereafter cited as *European*; for a more detailed examination of translations from this author, see my article, "The Prose Fiction of Baculard d'Arnaud in Late Eighteenth-Century England," *French Studies*, XVIII (April 1970), 1–18.
46. The *Universal*, his chief periodical purveyor, did, in fact, snip out a

stories appeared serially twenty-six times from 1766 to 1800; and eight of his works were translated as booklength publications, two being adapted by the celebrated Clara Reeve and Sophia Lee.

As indicated in the previous chapter, D'Arnaud, of all the French sentimental writers presented to the British public, underwent the most careful scrutiny when translators mined his work for new material. Nevertheless, even after their judicious selection of the more subdued domestic and historical tales and their omissions and expurgations of excessively lugubrious or bathetic material, more than enough melancholy, sentiment, and morality remained in the translated fiction to impress upon British readers D'Arnaud's talent in this particular sphere. The French critics, exposed of course to the totality of his work and familiar with all its aspects, were vociferously pro or con regarding his virtues and defects.[47] The English critics, robbed of his extravagancies by the translators, were generally tepid. For instance, the *Monthly* found *Warbeck* "indeed a *pathetic* tale; and the Reader of sensibility will be instructed and entertained by it,"[48] whereas the *Critical* felt that "the whole is not very interesting."[49] The *Analytical* commented à propos of *The Exiles*, "This improbable tale is tolerably well told, and comparatively speaking, has a little merit; but it is spun out to a

brief story and a footnote from the collection; entitled respectively "The New Clementina" and "The Character of Richardson," both were identified as by the "celebrated M. d'Arnaud" and printed in the December 1783 issue.

47. The *Année Littéraire*, always an enthusiastic partisan, praised without reservation his talent for exciting "cette douce sensibilité, expression du sentiment, qui arrache des larmes délicieuses aux coeurs les plus indifferens"— (1777), I, 216; he possessed that art by which "dans ses ouvrages le précepte coule doucement dans les coeurs et s'y imprime par des exemples"—(1770), VIII, 290. Less partisan (and more rational) critics like those of the *Correspondance littéraire*, deplored his penchant for the *lugubre et larmoyant*, precisely those qualities which seldom traveled across the channel. "Pourquoi prendre à tâche d'attrister les coeurs tendres," they said, "[avec] le tableau de toutes les peines et de tous les malheurs qui peuvent affliger l'humanité?"— article dated 1773 in *Correspondance littéraire, philosophique et critique de Grimm et Diderot*, VIII (Paris: Furne, 1830), 220–221, hereafter cited as *CL*.

48. *Monthly*, LXXV (August 1786), 153.

49. *Critical*, LX (November 1785), 395.

tedious length; and raises curiosity rather than interest."[50] And the *Critical*'s reviewer, after perusing *The History of Count Gleichen*, could only protest, "In short, this is a modern sentimental novel, plentifully adorned with ahs! and ohs! with little real pathos and less interest. Alice at last dies, in a fortunate moment, fortunate for Gleichen, for the reader, and supremely fortunate for the reviewer."[51] But to judge by the statistics concerning D'Arnaud's fictional appearances, public opinion heeded less the grumblings of the guardians of literary taste than the *European*'s advice that his "elegant compositions are replete with sentiment and sensibility; and we recommend them to the perusal of those ladies who aim at mental improvement."[52]

During the last fifteen years of the century another French writer enjoyed considerable popularity in England: the Chevalier de Florian. His career in translation had begun inauspiciously. *Les Six Nouvelles* were published in France in 1784, but not until 1786, when Mr. Robinson translated his works and several identified stories appeared in *Tales, Romances, Apologues, Anecdotes, and Novels*, did his work come before the English public. Even then, the stories borrowed by the magazines, like "Bathmendi," "Célestine" (retitled "Alphonso and Marina"), and "Sophronime," were published anonymously. Six years later the situation had changed considerably. *New Tales*, published in 1792 "From the French of M. de Florian," provided the magazines with a useful source of short fiction; they printed all but one of the stories and identified each as Florian's. "Claudine" was even exposed in three different and original translations. *Gonsalvo of Cordova*, also successful, appeared twice in book form and as a three-year serial in the *Lady's Magazine*. Rediscovering, moreover, *Tales, Romances, etc.* during the 1790's, the periodicals reprinted and acknowledged all of Florian's compositions.

50. *Analytical*, IV (June 1789), 221.
51. *Critical*, LXII (September 1786), 235–236.
52. *European*, IV (December 1783), 450.

Florian's celebrity during the nineties was very likely due to the critical reception which had greeted two intervening works, *Numa Pompilius* and *Estelle*. The *English Review* and the *Monthly*, which reviewed the French original of *Numa*, noted its resemblance to Fénélon's *Telemachus* and were not displeased with the result. "The duties of princes, and of simple individuals, are painted in the most amiable colours," said the former;[53] the latter praised its "purity of sentiments, elegant simplicity in the expression of those sentiments, and many other good qualities, which render a moral romance instructive and entertaining."[54] *Estelle*, twice translated, pleased equally—as, in fact, it had pleased the French, who tended to identify Florian with this work rather than with the *Nouvelles* or *Numa*.[55] The author's "imagery is chosen with great topical propriety, and his narration is highly polished," declared the *Monthly*;[56] the *Analytical* thought it "full of beautiful pictures" and composed in a style "elegant and flowery";[57] and the *European* assured its readers that "those who delight to read pastorals, will find entertainment in the present performance."[58]

The tone of the English criticism adequately indicates how facile and inoffensive sentimental prose fiction became under the pen of Florian. French critics had not been unaware of this pallidness. The *Correspondance littéraire* accorded to *Numa* "de la douceur, de la grace, de la facilité," but noted that the author "a beau chercher le ton épique, il retombe toujours dans celui de la romance et de l'eglogue." The same critic quoted with some approval the remark

53. *English Review; or, An Abstract of English and Foreign Literature*, IX (February 1787), 135, hereafter cited as *English*.

54. *Monthly*, LXXV (Appendix 1786), 513.

55. N. L. M. Désessarts, writing in 1800, noted, "Le succès de ce charmant ouvrage fut prodigieux, et s'est toujours soutenu depuis": *Les Siècles littéraires de la France, ou nouveau dictionnaire historique, critique et bibliographique de tous les écrivains français, morts et vivans, jusqu'à la fin du XVIIIᵉ siècle* (Paris: l'auteur, 1800), III, 81.

56. *Monthly*, n.s. XXV (February 1798), 213.

57. *Analytical*, II (October 1788), 253.

58. *European*, XXXIII (April 1798), 259.

by Marie Antoinette—a reader scarcely noted for literary percep-
tion, for she was very fond of D'Arnaud—that " 'En lisant *Numa*
. . . il m'a semblé que je mangeais de la soupe au lait.' "[59] Nevertheless, his works found popularity with English readers, perhaps, as
the *Gentleman's* suggested, because they felt sympathetic towards
a French novelist of noble birth who, though the victim of misfortune during the Revolution, could retain his lightness and optimism. At least that magazine remarked that "Amidst the dark
cloud in which France is now involved, where all whose curiosity
is directed to what passes in that wretched country have their attention fixed on scenes of cruelty and tales of murder, it is some consolation to catch at every passing ray which beams across the gloom
from Genius and from Virtue."[60]

Used to indigenous lady novelists, the British public did not
boggle about accepting the productions of celebrated French authoresses. The career of Mme Riccoboni might in fact be considered as important across the channel as on the continent. All of
her works were translated into English; her continuation of Marivaux's *Marianne* became a standard part of the English version of
that novel; and British critical opinion of her talent was generally
high. "On the whole, this Lady is a lively, agreeable writer," said
the *Monthly*, "and may rank with St. Aubin, and our famous Mrs.
Haywood: perhaps, too, with Mrs. Lennox, and Mrs. ——, who
translated the Letters of Ninon de L'Enclos."[61]

The History of the Marquis de Cressy had first been offered in
1759—"unsuccessfully," according to the *Monthly* in a review
of the second edition in 1765. *Letters from Juliet Lady Catesby*,
translated by Frances Brooke, appeared in 1760. Admitting they
might amuse "readers of a delicate, sentimental turn of mind," the

59. Article dated 1786, *CL*, XIII (Paris, 1831), 62.
60. *Gentleman's*, LXII (December 1792), 1128.
61. *Monthly*, XXXVIII (January 1768), 73. "Mrs. ——" was Elizabeth
Griffith and "St. Aubin," Penelope Aubin; it is interesting to note that all of
the English authoresses named had themselves done translations from the
French.

Monthly continued that "they are too destitute, however, both of narrative or humour, to be very generally admired."[62] This critical assessment proved totally erroneous: the novel was a solid seller with the British public, going through four editions by 1764 and a sixth in 1780. Subsequently, English translations of her novels appeared almost simultaneously with the French originals every year from 1764 to 1767 and in 1772, 1778, 1781, and 1784; and the magazines picked up shorter fiction like "The Blindman" and "Ernestina." Critical notices were almost invariably favorable, and most included extensive quotation.

Concerning Mme Riccoboni, the English and French critics were even more in accord than they had been about Marmontel. The French praised indefatigably her delicacy of sentiment, her naturalness of manner, and her moral perceptivity. Ease of style and "réflexions fines et justes," in the words of the *Correspondance littéraire*, were her hallmark;[63] and that journal, not given to extravagance, later commented that her novels "[ont transporté] nos jeunes femmes et nos gens du monde, sensibles à l'excès aux agrémens et aux détails pleins de grace et de délicatesse."[64] The English critics seemed to have borrowed their neighbors' pen. The *Letters from Lord Rivers* "unfold, with delicacy, many of the finer feelings of the heart, are enriched with just sentiments and are written with no inconsiderable degree of elegance and animation," according to the *Monthly*.[65] The *Critical* found in the *Letters from Elizabeth-Sophia de Valiere* "an almost uninterrupted profusion of generous sentiments";[66] indeed, the reviewer continued, "We are even of the opinion, that those who can peruse these letters without being greatly agitated by several passages must be void of sensibility."[67] English opinion, as well as French, easily concurred

62. *Monthly*, XXII (June 1760), 521.
63. Article dated 1764, *CL*, III (Paris, 1829), 491.
64. Article dated 1772, *CL*, VII (Paris, 1830), 428.
65. *Monthly*, LIX (September 1778), 233–234.
66. *Critical*, XXIV (July 1772), 63.
67. *Ibid.*, p. 65. At least one English reviewer found this talent used reprehensibly, however. Assessing *The History of Miss Jenny Salisbury*, the *Critical*

with Clara Reeve's judgment that Mme Riccoboni's "novels are first rate" (I, 132).

Equally esteemed by the British, but for slightly different reasons, was Mme de Genlis.[68] Translations were made of all her works and were warmly welcomed by the English audience. *Adelaide and Theodore* went through four editions between 1783 and 1796; the novel was serialized by both the *Universal* and the *Lady's*, and several of the interpolated stories found their way into other magazines. *Tales of the Castle* was a similar success: five editions between 1785 and 1798, as well as extracts in the periodicals. The later *Knights of the Swan* appeared in two different translations. Moreover, her shorter fiction was assembled in the flatteringly-titled *Beauties of Genlis* and by 1791 was enjoying a third edition.

A comparison of French and English criticism of Mme de Genlis' work reveals, interestingly enough, that her countrymen were somewhat more severe with her than the foreign observers. Some, like La Harpe, preferred the instruction rather than the amusement which she offered. To *Adèle et Théodore* she gave "une forme de roman, et y a mêlé beaucoup d'épisodes qui ne manquent pas d'intérêt; mais j'avoue que je suis moins content de cette partie que de celle qui est purement didactique," he said; "Plusieurs de ces épisodes sont trop longs, ne tiennent pas assez à l'objet principal, occupent trop de place et sont trop détaillés, si on ne les donne que comme des exemples."[69] The *Correspondance littéraire* concurred about *Adèle et Théodore*, believing she had "souvent gâté l'effet des

---

called it "a most incomparable bit of French cookery," full of "contemptible commonplace ingredients," but "so delicately seasoned" and "so disguised, that you eat away, and pronounce it to be excellent"; in his opinion, "this is an imposition of the most fatal tendency to youth, and that the more artfully it is managed, the more hurtful it is to genuine unsuspecting virtue": XVIII (October 1764), 313–314.

68. Magdi Wahba discusses her reception in "Madame de Genlis in England," *Comparative Literature*, XIII (summer 1961), 221–238.

69. Jean-François La Harpe, *Correspondance littéraire, adressée à son altesse Mgr le grand-duc, aujourd'hui empereur de Russie, et à M. le comte André Schowalow, Chambellan de l'imperatrice Catherine II, depuis 1774 jusqu'à 1789*, III (Paris: Migneret, 1801), 315.

situations les plus touchantes par des traits d'une sensibilité factice ou par des exagérations également froides et romanesques."[70] However, Grimm was more gallant about *Les Veillées:* "Si sa touche manque de chaleur et d'énergie, elle a de l'élégance et de la simplicité, quelquefois même des traits de naturel et de vérité, une sensibilité douce et touchante."[71]

Both her sensibility and her didacticism, however, delighted the English critics. Although some speculated nervously that *Adelaide and Theodore* might be a bit too French—"some of the descriptions of female manners in France," worried the *Monthly,* "will be thought by many to be, in a moral light, injudicious"[72]—they generally lauded, in the *Critical*'s words, "the general strictness and purity of its precepts, and the exquisite delicacy with which the most important lessons are inculcated."[73] She had the happy ability to combine pedagogy with fictional embellishment and morality with ease and elegance of style. The *Gentleman's* found *Tales of the Castle* "replete with sound sense and excellent precepts";[74] the *European* approved her intentions "to inform the mind and improve the heart, by diverting and pleasing the imaginations."[75] Her works were "deserving public honours, on the score of public utility," declared Clara Reeve; "I had rather be the author of such books as these, than be reckoned the first wit of the Age" (II, 99).[76]

70. Article dated 1782, *CL,* XI (Paris, 1830), 21.

71. Article dated 1784, *CL,* XII (Paris, 1830), 215.

72. *Monthly,* LXX (May 1784), 345. Mme de Genlis was the only prominent author besides Marmontel whose "Frenchness" gave pause to the critics, but they were not always in agreement whether it was good or bad. The *Critical,* in a generally favorable review, voiced an opinion similar to the *Monthly*'s about *Adelaide and Theodore*: "we dare not recommend them [the stories] to an English family without the exact attention of a careful mother, who possesses both sensibility and judgment to adapt them to our own customs": LVI (October 1783), 300; on the other hand, the *Gentleman's,* after perusing *Tales of the Castle,* found it "gay and pleasing, and *toute à la Françoise*": LX (February 1785), 130.

73. *Critical,* LVI (October 1783), 301.

74. *Gentleman's,* LX (February 1785), 130.

75. *European,* VII (January 1785), 42.

76. Reaction to her later novels was less uniformly favorable. The *Analytical* approved *Rash Vows,* for instance, but the *Monthly* felt the sentiments

The productions of Mme Le Prince de Beaumont, heavyhanded but morally impeccable, received little critical attention from the French, although Sabatier de Castres commended her ability "de placer l'érudition commune à propos, et de mettre en action, dans des fables ou des historiettes, des principes clairs et de sages leçons."[77] She is nevertheless entitled to a small niche in the translated literature of the period, for all of her major novels appeared in English, title pages almost always established her identity, and the principal critical journals of the time reviewed the majority of her works. Unlike Mesdames Riccoboni and de Genlis, however, she failed to win a significant reputation with the reading public, as two facts indicate: none of her novels ever had more than one edition, and none of her stories run by the *Lady's Magazine* was either acknowledged as hers or reprinted in any other journal.

It is difficult to attribute her lack of fame to anything other than a lack of talent—a deficiency which very likely the French critics were well aware of. She meant well, as the English realized, and her earnest moral instruction no doubt prompted the numerous translations of her works. The motivation for *The Triumph of Truth*, her best-received novel, was "so laudable, and in the execution, instruction and entertainment are so agreeably blended," according to the *Monthly*, "that it will, we doubt not, be very acceptable to the generality of readers."[78] But the reviewers cavilled at her general handling of stories and characters. Faced with *The Virtuous Widow*, the *Critical's* commentator "cannot help observing, that in all her works we scarcely meet with the character of a real man and woman, as they come from the hands of nature, with passions to influence and reason to direct them. . . . Every feeling they have puts their frame in agitation, harrows up their souls, and

---

"more forced, more unnatural; and the manners are more artificial": n.s. XXIX (August 1799), 467; and it found "tints of unnatural colouring" in *The Rival Mothers*: n.s. XXXVI (October 1801), 187.

77. Sabatier de Castres, *Les Trois Siècles de notre littérature, ou tableau de l'esprit de nos écrivains, depuis François I, jusqu'en 1772* (Amsterdam et Paris, 1772), III, 110.

78. *Monthly*, LII (June 1775), 507.

for some time deprives them of the use of reason"; he concluded, in short, "we cannot recommend the perusal of such novels to persons of either sex who have the misfortune to be of a solitary cast, or to have weak nerves."[79] More significantly, they unanimously objected to sentiments which "more than border on fanaticism," as the *Analytical* said of the *Letters of Mme du Montier*.[80] Atypical of most of the French sentimental novels, in which religion was treated sincerely but undogmatically, her works consistently promoted Catholicism, and the critics condemned her militancy. "All the virtuous agents in this romance are strict Roman Catholics," observed the *Critical* of *The New Clarissa*; "we wish the authoress . . . had left us more room to applaud her moderation."[81]

The last notable French sentimental author to win the attention of the English public was of course Bernardin de St.-Pierre. The furor with which *Paul et Virginie* was received in France was duplicated, albeit on a lesser scale, in England. Under its two English titles of *Paul and Mary* and *Paul and Virginia*, it went through nine editions and a magazine appearance between 1789 and 1800; in addition, Edward Augustus Kendall edited it for children in his collection *The Beauties of St. Pierre*, published in 1797 and again in 1799. Though less celebrated, *The Indian Cottage* was reprinted three times from 1791 to 1800, as well as appearing once in a journal. Furthermore, all of St.-Pierre's productions bore his name.

Contemporary French admiration of *Paul et Virginie* can be summarized no better than by the judgment of the *Correspondance littéraire*: "quelques simples qu'en soient tous les incidens," the novel "attache par une foule de tableaux neufs et intéressans, par les peintures les plus riches d'une nature presque inconnue, par

---

79. *Critical*, XXI (June 1766), 438–439.
80. *Analytical*, XXVI (July 1797), 77.
81. *Critical*, XXVI (November 1768), 355. Similar objections were made by the *Critical* to the *Letters of Mme du Montier* and by the *Monthly* to *The Virtuous Widow* and *Letters from Emerance to Lucy*. Clara Reeve noted this tendency but excused her: her "writings are strongly tinctured with bigotry and enthusiasm, but she always means to support the cause of virtue" (II, 38).

les développemens de la passion la plus douce et la plus naturelle, par l'expression soutenue d'un sentiment vif et profond."[82] Contemporary British opinion, though considerably less effusive, ranged from the favorable to the enthusiastic. Objecting mildly to "too much of the costume of polished life" and "a little error" in the natural history, the *Critical* did grant the story charm; it "will be peculiarly pleasing to readers, where soothing melancholy leads them to be fond of pathetic catastrophes."[83] The *European* was considerably more animated in describing its effects on the reader: "Genuine strokes of nature awaken the tenderest and most refined sensibilities of the human heart in almost every page of this chaste and simple, but deeply affecting story; and dispose the mind to imbibe, with equal advantage and delight, the precepts of true wisdom and sound morality with which the work abounds."[84] They and the *Gentleman's* particularly applauded—and quoted—the children's benevolence to the escaped Negro slave. Helen Maria Williams's later translation received only brief notice; but "Miss W's [sic] talents and taste, as a translator, will, however, to say the least, suffer no disparagement from comparison," according to the *Analytical*;[85] and the *Monthly* felt that a new translation of "the present exquisite tale" was not superfluous, since "few tales will better bear a repetition."[86]

Rousseau, Marmontel, Baculard d'Arnaud, Florian, Mesdames Riccoboni, de Genlis, and Le Prince de Beaumont, and St.-Pierre —these were the French sentimental authors best known to the English reading public through translations, both in book form and in serializations. That their popularity in England approached, if not equalled, that on the continent is made evident by the number of translations and reprints of their works; that the English critics' opinions corresponded in almost all instances with that of their continental counterparts suggests that critical standards were in-

82. Article dated 1788, *CL*, XIV (Paris, 1831), 103.
83. *Critical*, LXIX (February 1790), 120.
84. *European*, XVII (February 1790), 116.
85. *Analytical*, XXIV (July 1796), 68.
86. *Monthly*, n.s. XX (June 1796), 232.

deed very similar in the two countries. One further indication of the congruence of French and British sentimental literary taste in the late eighteenth century may be adduced: the reactions to three books which became bestsellers in both countries.

Mme de Graffigny's *Lettres d'une Péruvienne*, published in 1747, continued to charm her compatriots throughout the rest of the century. In the opinion of the *Nouvelle Bibliothèque d'un homme de goût*, it offered "tout ce que la tendresse a de plus vif, de plus doux et de plus touchant. C'est la nature embellie par le sentiment; c'est le sentiment lui-même qui s'exprime avec une élégante naiveté."[87] Although an early English translation had appeared in England in 1749, not until the later decades did Mme de Graffigny's novel come into its own in England. Six editions of the *Letters* in at least three different translations were welcomed by the British between 1760 and 1797, as well as complete reprints in two periodicals. The story was still affecting enough in 1774 to inspire a one-volume augmentation by R. Roberts; and the *Monthly* willingly reviewed her version, for "there is very considerable merit in the Peruvian letters; and we shall not, in any probability, ever have a better translation of them, than the present."[88]

Even though it did not like the work—definitely a minority opinion—the *Correspondance littéraire* could not refuse to acknowledge that Mme Elie de Beaumont's *Lettres du Marquis de Roselle* had "une sorte de succès; c'est qu'il est rempli de sentimens honnêtes et d'une sorte de morale à la portée de tout le monde; on y trouve même quelques sermons assez chauds."[89] The English critics and the English public were not so indifferent. "The sentiments are unaffectedly elegant, and its tendency unexceptionably moral," commended the *Critical*;[90] the *Monthly* hailed the authoress for treating "every circumstance and character with becoming delicacy and decorum."[91] More importantly, the *Critical* provided its read-

87. IV, 48.
88. *Monthly*, LI (August 1774), 162.
89. Article dated 1764, *CL*, IV (Paris, 1829), 20–21.
90. *Critical*, XIX (May 1765), 351.
91. *Monthly*, XXXI (Appendix 1764), 516.

ers with four pages of quotation, the *Monthly* with eight; and popular demand called forth two editions.

Mme de Montolieu's *Caroline de Litchfield*, though it excited little critical comment in France, was by no means ignored by the public: three editions in 1786, and others in 1787 and 1789. Nor did the translation go unheeded in England. Although ignorant of the authoress's name, the English audience bestowed its favor immediately, and the novel had two editions in 1786–87, one more in 1795, and long reviews, one of five pages in the *Critical*. The *Monthly* recommended "the work, as by far the most ingenious and pathetic of the kind, that hath been for many years imported from the continent";[92] and the *Critical* welcomed "this pleasing author to our island. . . . It is her first visit; but we hope her reception will be sufficiently flattering to induce her again to appear in another form."[93]

To this point, it has been the contention that two facts indicate the degree of British acceptance of translations of French sentimental fiction: the critics' comments, in general favorable; and the number of appearances which the works made before the British public. But until now, these facts have been examined only with reference to well-known authors or to individual best sellers. Have they any relevance to that mass of anonymous or semianonymous translations offered to the public by their earnest interpreters? They do indeed, to this extent: that the critics, though they frequently bewailed the "Frenchness" of the translations, reviewed them without discrimination and accorded to them proportionally at least as much space as they gave to English fiction; and that despite such conservative and patriotic grumbling, translations of ordinary foreign fiction continued to proliferate decade by decade.

Regarding the criticism, it is undeniable that, in spite of the fact that some commentators found the French novelists superior to the English in their delineation of character and sentiment, hostility and suspicion frequently greeted new translations. Many critics

92. *Monthly*, LXXVI (March 1787), 266.
93. *Critical*, LXII (September 1786), 203.

were inclined to believe that a translation, depicting as it did foreign and "too French" customs, would have little appeal for the British public.[94] They attacked what they considered to be frivolity. The *Monthly*, for example, found all but one of the stories in *Favourite Tales* "light and trifling; and *one* is of the *free and easy* kind. Productions like the present are extremely numerous on the continent, but we wish not to see them encouraged here. The *verbiage*, the frothiness of a Parisian *petit-maître*, is in no way suitable to honest John Bull."[95]

Somewhat more seriously, the critics charged the translations with introducing an immorality typically French to the British public. They became preoccupied by the possibility that overly-warm descriptions of passion and vice might so enthrall the reader that he would neglect the ultimate lesson that happiness comes through virtue alone. The *Critical*'s discussion of Dorat's *Fatal Effects of Inconstancy* well exemplifies this attitude. "The galantries of the beau monde in France are so delineated [in this novel], as to make such descriptions improper for young people," said the reviewer; "the misfortunes of two sinners who still retain their love in the highest degree, incline us, on account of that love, to commiserate their condition; and we are less apt to be shocked at their crimes, than to wish they had escaped with impunity"; such sympathy with vice was not to be encouraged, and the critic "would sooner put into the hands of our sons and daughters Prior's loosest tale, than the soft, enchanting descriptions which are apt

94. Still, there were some who were disposed to be broad-minded about the issue. The anonymous *Louis de Boncoeur* was described thus by the *Monthly*: "The characters and manners being French, may appear extravagant to merely English readers; but even they will, on the whole, be considerably pleased with this performance; for it is superior to our common novels, both in its composition and tendency": n.s. XIX (March 1796), 453–454. The *Critical* advised that if the "proper allowances" were made for the foreign character of Gorjy's *Blansay*, it "will stand high in our catalogue of novels": LXIX (March 1790), 35.

95. *Monthly*, LXXVIII (June 1788), 531. Similar objections were made to Masson de Morvillier's *Adelaide* and, more severely, to Louvet de Couvrai's *Life and Adventures of the Chevalier de Faublas* and *Emily de Varmont*.

to be met with in the present performance."[96] It was feared also that sentiment, mishandled, might overstep considerably the bounds of propriety. For example, the *Analytical* would not recommend *Zelia in the Desert*, by Mme Daubenton, to its readers, "as we do not wish our fair countrywomen to imbibe such overstrained notions of love; the two extremes too frequently meet, and the grossest sensuality often lies concealed under double refined sentiments."[97]

And even when they made no objections to the morality, the English critics often protested against the "extravagance" of the stories, meaning by that an overabundance of sentiment, trivial emotion, and drama. The *"prettinesses, the sensibilities"* of Gorjy's *Louis and Nina* annoyed the *Monthly*, as they did the *Analytical*; "In these most *dismal* tales, sentimental to the very marrow," complained the latter, "the tender feelings are torn to tatters, and the shreds vaingloriously displayed. Sudden death, everlasting love, methodical madness, bad weather, a breaking heart, putrid body, worn out night cap, etc. etc. Nothing but sentiment!"[98]

Nevertheless, although this hostility was indeed typical of one current of criticism, when weighed with general critical reaction it counterbalanced but did not overwhelm the favorable comments made about well-known authors and other anonymous transla-

96. *Critical*, XXXVIII (November 1774), 393. The reviewer preferred to Dorat's work *The Child of Nature, Improved by Chance*, a novel spuriously attributed to Helvétius, whose "pictures are drawn with a luxurious fancy, and prudery, it is probable, will condemn them; but they are too well intended on that account": XXXVIII (October 1774), 270. Amusingly enough, this novel was also issued with a lengthy title implying it was pornographic (see bibliography); whatever the reason for its popularity, Paul Kaufman records in *Borrowings from the Bristol Library* that it was the only other translation from the French in the library and in frequency of times borrowed it stood twenty-fifth in a list of 238 Belles Lettres titles.

97. *Analytical*, IV (June 1789), 221. Framéry's *Memoirs of the Marquis de St. Forlaix*, Charlotte Smith's translation of Prévost's *Manon Lescaut*, and Rutledge's *Julia* were censured for similar reasons.

98. *Analytical*, IV (June 1789), 222. Condemned on the same ground were Dubois-Fontanelle's *The Effects of the Passions*, Beaurieu's *The Man of Nature*, and particularly the overly *sensible* hero of Loaisel de Tréogate's *Julius or the Natural Son*.

tions. Moreover, several other aspects of late eighteenth-century criticism as a whole are worth noting. For instance, during those four decades of interest in translations from the French, no pattern of critical approval or disapproval of them is discernible. One finds praise and blame mixed as often during the 1760's as during the 1780's; and even the French Revolution provoked no outbursts against pernicious foreign literature, although the *Monthly*'s reviews became unusually waspish during 1793 and 1794. To judge by the general tenor of the critics' remarks and the space accorded to them in the periodicals, the fact that French sentimental literature was entering in quantity on the British literary scene went almost unnoticed, and critics of literature treated the translations as a normal part of their profession. No outcries of "Another French novel!" or "Vitiation of native literature!" were heard; and if the critics were sometimes harsh towards a book for being too French, as often as not they were willing to accord more space to the reviews, with quotation, of foreign works than of indigenous ones.[99]

Critics' remarks, though instructive, are seldom definitive gauges of a genre's popularity: more significant are those statistics which detail printings and reprintings and thereby bear concrete witness to the public interest. When one examines the figures on publication and reprints of anonymous or semianonymous works only—in other words, figures excluding appearances of works by those major authors already discussed—it is clear that by themselves they reflect the pattern of curiosity and enthusiasm described previously in chapter 2. From 1760 to 1769, six novels and nine

99. A portion of the *Monthly*'s review of D'Auvigny's *Memoirs of Madame Barneveldt* is worth quoting for its rarity—and the date should be noted: "it may reasonably be expected that no book should be translated, which does not possess considerable intrinsic merit; yet it has happened that the depravity of public taste, or the defective judgment of individuals, has considerably augmented our native stock of indifferent performances, by importations of foreign works which seldom prove to be valuable acquisitions, even to the circulating libraries": n.s. XVIII (November 1795), 345. It should be mentioned that German literature was also being translated in quantity during the same period.

stories appeared; from 1770 to 1779, nineteen of the former and eighteen of the latter; from 1780 to 1789, twenty-seven and forty-six. Statistics for the nineties emphatically repeat that curious disparity between serial and hardcover publication noted before. The periodicals published only fifteen stories, all but three of them between 1790 and 1794. The booksellers produced thirty-five translations, with twenty-four appearing in the last six years. Notwithstanding the situation during the last decade, however, the figures for these works by minor writers prove that celebrated foreign authors were clearly not the only attraction which drew the British public to translated French stories; the genre of sentimental prose fiction had its own innate appeal.

The disappearance of translations from the magazines after 1795 suggests very strongly that in one area at least, the vogue of sentimental French fiction in England had come to an end; periodicals have always been obliged to be as topical and current as possible to attract readers successfully. The large number of hardcover translations during the nineties would seem to show, nevertheless, that novel readers—perhaps the patrons of the rapidly-growing circulating libraries—had not lost their appetite for sentimental fare, and it is worth noting that almost every booklength translation published during the 1790's came from fiction written before 1789 or during the Revolution's early years. Most were reprints of earlier successes, like Marmontel's *Moral Tales* and Rousseau's *Eloisa*, but even the original translations were drawn from older works. Miss Gunning took the *Memoirs of Madame Barneveldt* from a 1732 novel by D'Auvigny; Helen Maria Williams re-did *Paul et Virginie*; Sénac de Meilhan's 1790 *Les Deux Cousins* became *The Cousins of Schiras*; Mme Le Prince de Beaumont's *Letters of Madame du Montier* dated from 1758; *Letters Written from Lausanne* came from Mme de Charrière's novel of 1788. The exceptions to this trend have their own interest. Three of Mme de Genlis' later works were translated, all more blatantly melodramatic than her earlier fiction. Two novels about the Revolution appeared, Gorjy's *Sentimental Tablets of the Good Pamphile*, originally written in 1791, and Fiévée's *Suzette's Dowry*, written in 1798; both recounted the tribulations of virtue during the debacle, a sentimental subject sentimentally treated by both.[100]

The eventual fate of translated French fiction was ultimately linked at the turn of the century with the fortunes of indigenous sentimental literature which, though it by no means disappeared at once from the market-place, was gradually declining in popularity.[101] That the genre should finally begin to lose its appeal is scarcely surprising; after thirty-five years the reading public had become only too familiar with sentimental themes and situations. Moreover, the satirists were finding it a good target for lampooning; writers like William Beckford in *Modern Novel Writing* (1796), Mary Charlton in *Rosella, or Modern Occurrences* (1799), and Maria Edgeworth in *Angelina* (1801) mocked both the stylistic excesses of sentimentality and the delusions it offered the reader.[102]

More important, a new challenger for public favor had entered the literary scene: the Gothic novel. In 1794 the *Analytical* offered a rather lengthy but instructive explanation for the shift in popular taste. Observing that "the too frequent reiteration of similar im-

100. For instance, in *Sentimental Tablets* (London, 1795), the young peasant who dismays his parents by going off with the revolutionaries finally repents such a mad step and returns home; he gives as the reasons for his foolish departure "disgust I felt at my condition in life" and "writings which I read with avidity, [and which] finished my seduction" (p. 120). The heroine of *Suzette's Dowry* (London, 1799) is also a young peasant who, thanks to a generous noblewoman, marries a bourgeois who makes a fortune during the Revolution; her new wealth permits her to rescue her benefactress from distress, but, she confesses, "ah! if ever I am at liberty to follow my own inclinations, it is in mediocrity I shall seek, not happiness, there is none for me, but tranquillity and self-enjoyment" (p. 175).

101. Two modern scholars discuss this particular problem: Winfield Rogers in "The Reaction against Melodramatic Sentimentality in the English Novel, 1796–1830," *PMLA*, XLIX (March 1934), 98–122; and W. F. Gallaway, who dates the reaction even earlier, in "The Conservative Attitude toward Fiction, 1770–1830," *PMLA*, LV (December 1940), 42–59. Both, however, as the titles of their articles indicate, show that sentimental literature did indeed endure into the 1800's.

102. Perhaps Jane Austen's *Sense and Sensibility* (1811) should also be added, for the first draft, *Elinor and Marianne*, was written about 1795.

pressions" dulls the mind, the commentator found that it becomes "necessary, in order to preserve the same degree of irritation, to be continually increasing the stimulating force." Fiction follows this principle. So that authors "may keep pace with the progress of fastidiousness in taste, [novels] must gradually ascend from the most simple exhibition of natural sentiments and passions, through every stage of splendid ornament, and wild extravagance." Deriving from this principle the explanation for "the present daily increasing rage for novels addressed to the strong passions of wonder and terrour," he speculated that "the class of readers, for whom this kind of entertainment is provided, as if no longer capable of deriving pleasure from the gentle and tender sympathies of the heart, require to have their curiosity excited by artificial concealments, their astonishment kept awake by a perpetual succession of wonderful incidents, and their very blood congealed with chilling horrors."[103]

The Gothic novel was, in fact, the very legitimate heir to the established traditions of sentimental fiction. The hero (or heroine) whose delicate sensibility already inclined him to tremble and to suffer more keenly than others; settings which, though they were to become progressively more gloomy and more menacing, were at a distance, either in time or in space, from common, civilized locales; the insistence that virtue, seeking only to live obediently according to the precepts of nature, would be continually persecuted by unnatural or malevolent forces—these were absorbed with no difficulty by the writers of Gothic romance, who simply added to them more mystery, more terror, and more wonderment.[104]

Sentimental fiction did not, thus, disappear; it was absorbed into a developing genre which offered more excitement and more novelty to the eager British audience. Yet translations from the

103. *Analytical*, XX (Appendix 1794), 489.

104. Tompkins, Foster, and Baker all thus see French sentimental translations as important contributors to this genre in England; the first cites in particular D'Arnaud, Mme de Genlis, and Framéry. In addition, Miss Tompkins indicates that certain ideas in French sentimental fiction may also be found in novels of social protest, such as those by Godwin and Holcroft.

French had played their own role in the development of British literature. Though they had no great significant influence on any notable English novelist, they did at least prepare the English public for further developments, at the same time that they interested and entertained it with their pictures of sensibility and benevolence. In doing so, translated French sentimental prose fiction contributed to a continuum of literary development which was to be sustained more effectively, in a way, across the channel than in the country which had produced it.

CHAPTER FOUR. FRENCH SENTIMENTAL AUTHORS AND THEIR WORKS IN ENGLISH TRANSLATION, 1760–1800

The following bibliography has been provided for three reasons: first, to supply bibliographical details which, while significant, were deliberately omitted from the text to avoid further encumbering it; second, to permit instant reference to the French authors whose works appeared in English; third, to establish definitively the French sources of English translations, a task heretofore neglected because of the complexity involved in correlating the two versions.

The sources of information for the translations and their French originals are numerous. Compiling a list of the English works involved principally Andrew Block, *The English Novel, 1740–1850*, 2nd ed. (London: Dawson, 1961); Dorothy Blakey, *The Minerva Press, 1790–1820* (Oxford: Bibliographical Society at the University Press, 1939); Montague Summers, *A Gothic Bibliography* (London: Fortune Press, 19—); Robert Mayo, *The English Novel in the Magazines, 1740–1815* (Evanston: Northwestern University Press, 1962); and *French Works in English Translation. A Bibliographical Catalogue, 1760–69* and *1770–79*, ed. J. A. R. Séguin (Jersey City: Ross Paxton, 1966). Identifying the French originals was accomplished with the help of Jules Gay, *Bibliographie des ouvrages relatifs à l'amour, aux femmes, et au mariage*. 4 vols. (Paris: Lemonnyer, 1894–1900); Angus Martin, "A First Listing of New French Prose Fiction, 1784–1788," *Australian Journal of French Studies*, IV (1966), 109–131; Daniel Mornet's bibliography of fiction in the first volume of his edition of Rousseau's *La Nouvelle Héloïse*, ed. "Grands Ecrivains de France" (Paris: Hachette, 1925); and André Monglond, *La France révolutionnaire. Annales de bibliographie et description des livres illustres*. 9 vols. (Grenoble: Arthaud, 1930–60). In addition, I have added new titles, both of book-length and of magazine fiction, whenever I have happened upon them.

The resultant bibliography contains, in many cases, a modification of the evidence in these sources, based on my own comparisons of the English and French versions. All novels and stories which I have personally seen are marked with an asterisk; they are to be found in the Bibliothèque Nationale, the Bibliothèque de l'Arsenal, the British Museum, or the New York Public Library. Those works which I did not examine are followed by the source, given in brackets, where I found them cited.[1] In a few cases I have connected French and English works when, although I saw only one, contemporary reviews or descriptions made the attribution reasonably sure. I have also quoted briefly translators' remarks about the source of their subject.

The bibliography is arranged in the following manner. A list of anonymous translations—anonymous either because I could not identify the French author or because I discovered neither the foreign author nor the French original—is given first; the English titles are listed alphabetically. A group of anthologies, also in alphabetical order, appears next. Wherever possible, the contents of each are enumerated; and when an anthologized translation of a significant French author was frequently reprinted by the periodicals, I have indicated in brackets a "see" reference to the author. Third comes the major portion of the bibliography: each French

---

1. The sole source for all serialized translations is Mayo; I have thus omitted listing his name. Besides Block, Blakey, and Summers, the following provided further information about translated novels: lists of new publications found in contemporary journals, like the *Analytical Review*, the *Gentleman's Magazine*, and the *Monthly Review*; catalogues of libraries like the British Museum and the Library of Congress; W.H. McBurney, *English Prose Fiction 1700–1800 in the University of Illinois Library* (Urbana: University of Illinois Press, 1965); and the *New Cambridge Bibliography of English Literature, 1660–1800*, ed. George Watson (Cambridge: University Press, 1971), abbreviated *NCBEL* in the text. Further titles were provided by John Clapp in his article "An Eighteenth-Century Attempt at a Critical Review of the Novel: the *Bibliothèque universelle des Romans*," *PMLA*, XXV (March 1910), 60–96; and all information on translations of Rousseau comes from James Warner's articles cited above in note 24, chapter 3.

author, followed by the alphabetically-listed titles of each French work, whether it be novel or story, and the complete titlepages of the English translations of it.[2] A work's appearances in periodicals are given after booklength translations; if quotations included in critical reviews exceeded five hundred words, I have counted them as periodical appearances.[3] A "likewise" preceding a magazine citation indicates a reprint of that work under the same translated title; an "also" indicates the same story or novel with a differently translated title.

It is hoped that this bibliography will serve to unite, in a reasonably definitive way, the English translations with their French originals and to indicate thereby the extent of the late eighteenth-century British reading public's acquaintance with contemporary French sentimental prose fiction.

ANONYMOUS

*"The Characters of Prévôt, Le Sage, Richardson, Fielding, and Rousseau. From the French of *La Jolie Femme; ou, la Femme du jour*: An entertaining Novel, published at Lyons, 1769," *Gentleman's*, XL (October 1770).

Confessions of a Beauty. From the French. London: Lane, 1798 [Blakey suggests the translator may be Mrs. Croffts].

The Count de Rethel: an Historical Novel. Taken from the French. 3 vols. London: Hookham, 1779; also *The Count de Rathel: An Historical Novel. Taken from the French.* London: Hookham, 1785 [Summers].

"La Dame généreuse," *Lady's*, XIII (March-October 1782)–XIV

2. In some cases, I was unable to find the French original from which a translation was taken; I have thus indicated in brackets "French original unidentified" and listed the English title alphabetically among the French works. Helvétius and Rousseau posed a slightly different problem, for each had spurious works attributed to him; I have noted in brackets, in these instances, "French original non-existent."

3. To simplify the citations, I have abbreviated somewhat the names of the commonest periodicals. Thus, *Universal* means the *Universal Magazine of Knowledge and Pleasure*; *Gentleman's* the *Gentleman's Magazine*; *Lady's* the *Lady's Magazine*, etc. Complete titles of all periodicals, small and large, are to be found in Mayo.

(May, July 1783) [story given in French]; also "La Dame généreuse. Translated from the French," *Lady's*, XIV (February, May 1783) [translation of the previously published French story]; also "The Generous Lady. Translated from the French," *Hibernian Magazine* (June-July 1783).

"The Danger of the Passions. An Allegorical Tale," *Universal Museum*, n.s. V (November-December 1769) [the first appearance of John Murdoch's translation and later gathered into his anthology *Pictures of the Heart*; see ANTHOLOGIES].

Durval and Adelaide. A Novel. By Catherine Lara. London: Ridgeway, 1796 [identified as a translation by both the *Analytical* and the *Monthly*].

"The Fatal Effects of Revenge. From the French," *Court Miscellany*, IV (July-September 1768).

The Foresters. A Novel Adapted from the French. By Miss Gunning. 4 vols. London: Low, 1796 [Block].

*"Heroick Virtue, or Love and Duty Reconciled. A Moral Tale, from the French," *London Magazine*, L (April-May 1781) [translated "For the *London Magazine*"]; likewise *Weekly Miscellany* (Sherborne), XVI (August-September 1781).

*"The History of Alsaleh, an Eastern Courtier (From *Pictures of the Heart, sentimentally delineated*, in 2 vols. 12 mo.)," *Universal*, LXXIII (October-November 1782) [from Murdoch's anthology; see ANTHOLOGIES]; likewise *Hibernian Magazine* (November-December 1783).

"History of Francis Count Montgomery and the Sieur d'Anglade. Translated from the French," *Court Miscellany*, II (September-October 1766).

*"The History of Okano: The Fragment of a Voyage to St. Domingo. (From the French of the *Mercure de France*.)," *Universal*, LXXXIII (September 1788).

The Innocent Rivals, a Novel; taken from the French, with Alterations and Additions. By a Lady. 3 vols. London: Bew, 1786 [*Monthly*].

The Invisible Man; or Duncam Castle. A Novel from the French. 2 vols. London: Lane, 1800 [Blakey].

Leonora. Translated by Mary Julia Young. London [?], 1796 [Summers ascribes the French original to Berthier].

Louis de Boncoeur, a domestic tale. By Catherine Lara. Translated from the French. 2 vols. London: Ridgeway, 1796 [*Analytical*].

**Love at First Sight. A Novel. From the French. With alterations and* *additions by Mrs.* [Susannah] *Gunning.* 5 vols. London: Lowndes, 1797.

The Misfortunes of Love. A novel translated from the French. London: Lane, 1785 [Blakey].

The Monk of the Grotto; or, Eugenio and Virginia. A Tale. From the French. 2 vols. London: Lane, 1800 [Blakey; a translation of *Eugenio et Virginia.* 2 vols. Paris, An VIII (1800)].

"Le Nourisson, Translated from the French by Wm Sh-w," *New Lady's,* II (October 1787)–III (April 1788); likewise *Gentleman's and London* (Dublin) (May-August 1788).

"Osman, or Modern Gratitude, Translated by a Lady," *Lady's,* IV (July-August 1773).

*"The Penitent Daughter, A Moral Tale. Translated from the French," *Caledonian Magazine; or, Aberdeen Repository,* I (June 1787).

"The Rival Princes, A Novel, Translated from the French. By J. W. Q——y," *Lady's,* XXIII (February-Supplement 1792)–XXIV (April-May 1793).

*"Rural Probity. A Tale. Translated from the French," *London,* XLII (August 1773) [translated "For the *London Magazine*"].

*"The Self-Rival. A nouvellette from the French," *Lady's,* XXI (March 1790).

"The Sentimental Coquette, a Fragment, from the French," *Sentimental Magazine,* I (November 1773)–II (January 1774).

*"The Sylph, an Entertaining Story, from the French," *London,* XLIX (November 1780); likewise *Hibernian Magazine* (December-Appendix 1780); likewise *Weekly Miscellany* (Sherborne), XVI (June 1781).

"The Wedding Interrupted, A Novel. Translated from the French," *Universal,* XVII (November 1765); likewise *Weekly Miscellany* (Sherborne), XI (February 1779); likewise *Moral and Entertaining,* IV (March 1779); likewise *Hibernian Magazine* (May-June 1779).

*"What an Escape! A Parental Lesson. (From the French of the *Mercure de France*)," *Universal,* LXXXIV (May 1789).

ANTHOLOGIES

The Country-Seat, or, Summer Evenings Entertainments. Translated from the French. 2 vols. London: Lowndes, 1762 [includes the following stories: Vol. I, "The History of Don Pedro d'Aguilar," "Innocence Preserved," "Arnold and Claramond," "Remarkable

Account of Three Prostitutes," "Melchu Kina," "The Self-Rival," and "Constant Love"; Vol. II, "The Loves of Cherea and Calirrhoe," "Efforts of Love and Friendship," and "Zora and Philamite, or Conjugal Fidelity"].

Favourite Tales. Translated from the French. London: Robinson, 1787 [includes, among others, "The Queen of Golconda" by the Chevalier de Boufflers, "Imerice, or, The Child of Nature" by the abbé Dulaurens, and a "Tale in the Manner of Sterne" and "The Mad Girl of St. Joseph's," both by the Chevalier de Grave; the *Gentleman's*, which reviewed the book in December 1787, also reprinted the last-named story].

Miscellanies in Prose and Verse, selected from the works of Marmontel and other celebrated authors. 2 vols. London, 1778 [*Monthly*].

A New and Complete Collection of Interesting Romances and Novels; Translated from the French, By Mr. Porney, Teacher of the French Language at Richmond, Surrey. London, n.d. [prints dated 1780; Clapp].

A New Volume of knowledge and entertainment, being translations of . . . the Bibliotheque Universelle des Romans. London, 1780 [Clapp].

*Original Essays and Translations. By Different Hands. Edinburgh: Balfour and Dickson, 1780 [contains, among other stories, "The History of Sarah Th—— (Translated from the French)," by St.-Lambert; translations done by William Richardson and Archibald Archer]; **Original Tales, Histories, Essays and Translations. By different Hands.* Edinburgh: Elliot, 1785.

*Pictures of the Heart, sentimentally delineated in The Danger of the Passions, an allegorical tale; The Adventures of a Friend of Truth, an oriental History, in two parts. The Embarrassments of Love, a Novel: and The Double Disguise, a drama in two acts. 2 vols. Dublin, 1783 [translated by John Murdoch, who says of the first two works, "For the hints, and little more than the hints, which gave birth to these compositions, I confess myself to have been, for several years, indebted to two fugitive French *morceaux*, of which I never could learn the authors," p. vi]; London, 1783 [British Museum].

Select Passages from the Most Celebrated French Authors. 1772 [Watt, *Bibliotheca Britannica*, Edinburgh, 1824].

*Sketches of the Lives and Writings of the Ladies of France, by Mrs. [Anne Ford] *Thicknesse.* 3 vols. London: Dodsley, 1780 [for reprints of *Inès de Cordoue*, see BERNARD].

*Tales, Romances, Apologues, Anecdotes, and Novels; humourous, sa-
tiric, entertaining, historical, tragical and moral; from the French
of the abbé Blanchet, M. Bret, M. de la Place, M. Imbert, M. Saint
Lambert, and the Chevalier de Florian. 2 vols. London: Robinson,
1786 [for reprints of "Bathmendi" and "The Constant Lovers,"
see FLORIAN; for reprints of "Sarah Phillips," see SAINT-LAMBERT].

ARCQ, PHILIPPE AUGUSTE DE SAINTE-FOIX, Chevalier D', b. 1721

*Le Palais du silence, conte philosophique. 2 vols. Amsterdam, 1754:
The Palace of Silence: A Philosophic Tale. Translated from the
French by a Lady. 2 vols. London: Bew, 1775 [Block].

ARNAUD, FRANÇOIS MARIE THOMAS DE BACULARD D', 1718–1805

*"Clary, ou le retour à la vertu récompensé," Les Epreuves du senti-
ment. Vol. I. Paris, 1772: *"The History of Rosetta. Translated
from the French of D'Arnaud," London, XLII (January-February
1773); likewise Hibernian Magazine (February-March 1773).
Le Comte de Comminge: See TENCIN.
*"Le Comte de Gleichen," Nouvelles historiques. Vol. III. Paris, 1777:
*The History of Count Gleichen, A German nobleman, who re-
ceived permission from Pope Gregory IX to have two wives at the
same time. Translated from the French of Arnaud. London: Hookham, 1786.
*"D'Almanzi," Suite des épreuves du sentiment. Vol. IV. Paris, 1776:
*The Exiles; or, Memoirs of the Count de Cronstadt. By Clara Reeve,
Author of The Old English Baron, Two Mentors, etc. 3 vols. Lon-
don: Hookham, 1788; *"Raymond and Clementina: A Moral Tale.
Illustrated with a beautiful Engraving of an interesting scene,
designed by Moreau," Universal, LXI (October 1777) [unac-
knowledged as D'Arnaud's].
*"Daminvile," Suite des épreuves du sentiment. Vol. V. Paris, 1778:
"Military Distress, or Daminville, an Anecdote," Lady's, X (Feb-
ruary 1779)–XI (April 1780) [unacknowledged as D'Arnaud's].
*Les Epoux malheureux, ou mémoires de M. et Mme de la Bedoyère.
Paris, 1745; augmented edition, 1785: The Unfortunate Attach-
ment; or, Memoirs of Mr. and Mrs. De La Bedoyere. 2 vols. Lon-
don: Vernor, 1794 [Summers].
*Les Epreuves du sentiment. Paris, 1772–79: The Tears of Sensibility.
Translated from the French. By J. Murdoch. 2 vols. 1773 [Block;
includes "The Cruel Father" ("Anne Bell"), "Rosetta, or the Fair
Penitent" ("Clary"), "Sidney and Silli, or the Man of Benevolence

and the Man of Gratitude" ("Sidney et Volsan"), and "The Rival Friends" ("Adelson et Salvini")]; 1783 [with two new pieces; NCBEL].

*Fanni, ou l'heureux repentir, histoire angloise. Londres, 1764: *Fanny, or Injur'd Innocence. London: Becket, 1766; Fanny, or, the Happy Repentance. From the French. Dublin, 1777 [Block]; *"Fanny, or the Happy Repentance. From the French of M. D'Arnaud," Universal, XXXIX (July 1766) [taken from the translation published by Becket]; likewise Weekly Miscellany (Sherborne), XV (December 1780-January 1781); also "The Happy Repentance, or Memoirs of Lord Whatley," Bouquet, II, Nos. 7–9 (January-March 1796).

*"Julie, anecdote historique," Les Epreuves du sentiment. Vol. I. Paris, 1772: *"Julia, or the Penitent Daughter, an Affecting History," Universal, LXX (February-March 1782) [acknowledged as D'Arnaud's in the introductory note; this story was preceded in the January 1782 Universal by a letter from a "Female Penitent" to D'Arnaud and his reply, both of which prompted the appearance of "Julia"]; likewise Hibernian Magazine (March-May 1782); likewise Weekly Entertainer, I (June 1783); also "Julia, or the Penitent Daughter. A Tale, from the French of M. Arnaud," Lady's, XXIV (1793).

*"Makin," Suite des épreuves du sentiment. Vol. IV. Paris, 1776: *"The Desert Island, or the Happy Recovery, a Tale, illustrated with a beautiful Engraving of an interesting Scene, designed by Monnet," Universal, LXII (April 1778) [the last paragraph acknowledges "M. de Arnaud, a celebrated French writer, from whom the above little history is chiefly taken"].

*"La Nouvelle Clémentine," Délassemens de l'homme sensible, ou anecdotes diverses. Vol. I. Paris, 1783: *"The New Clementina: An Affecting History (From the French of the celebrated M. d'Arnaud)," Universal, LXXIII (December 1783); *"The Character of Richardson (By the celebrated M. d'Arnaud)," Universal, LXXIII (December 1783) [taken from a footnote in the French story].

*"Le Prince de Bretagne," Nouvelles historiques. Vol. II. Paris, 1777: *"The Prince of Brittany, a New Historical Novel, by the Author of 'The Lord of Crequi,'" Universal, LXXVI (March-June 1785); likewise Hibernian Magazine (April-September 1785); likewise Weekly Entertainer, IX (June 1787)–X (July 1787).

*"Salisbury," Nouvelles historiques. Vol. I. Paris, 1774: *"Edward III

and the Countess of Salisbury. An Historical Novel, Never before Published," *Universal*, LV (November-December 1774).

*"Sidney et Volsan, histoire anglaise," *Les Epreuves du sentiment*. Vol. II. Paris, 1772: *The History of Sidney and Volsan. Translated from the French of the celebrated Arnaud*. Dublin, 1772; *"Benevolence and Gratitude, a Novel," *Sentimental Magazine*, III (October-December 1775) [unacknowledged as D'Arnaud's]; likewise *Caledonian Magazine and Review*, II (November 1783).

*"Le Sire de Créqui," *Nouvelles historiques*. Vol. I. Paris, 1774: *"The Lord of Crequi, a New Historical Novel. From the French of the celebrated M. D'Arnaud," *Universal*, LXXI (October-November 1782)– LXXII (January 1783); likewise *Caledonian Magazine and Review*, I (April-May 1783); likewise *New London*, II (January-April 1786); likewise *Gentleman's and London* (Dublin) (March-May 1786); likewise *Berwick Museum*, II (June 1786)–III (January 1787).

*"Varbeck," *Nouvelles historiques*. Vol. I. Paris, 1774: *Warbeck: a Pathetic Tale. Translated from the original French by the author of The Recess* [Sophia Lee]. 2 vols. London: Lane, 1786 [Block; NCBEL in one place lists 1785, in another 1786]; *rptd. Dublin, 1786; "Warbeck," *Oxford Magazine*, XIII (December 1776); also "Warbeck, an Historical Novel, from the French of Mr. Arnaud," *Sentimental Magazine*, V (August-October 1777); likewise *Monthly Miscellany*, V (August-September 1777).

AUVIGNY, Jean du Castre d', 1712–1743

Mémoires de Madame de Barneveldt. 2 vols. Paris, 1732 [a contemporary note in the Arsenal's copy affirms Auvigny's authorship]: *Memoirs of Madame Barneveldt. Translated from the French by Miss Gunning*. 2 vols. London, 1795.

BARTHELEMY, Jean Jacques, 1716–1795

Les Amours de Carite et Polydore, roman traduit du grec. Paris, 1760: *Charite and Polydorus. To which is prefixed a Treatise on Morals. With the life of the Author*. London: Otridge, 1799 [NCBEL]; *Charite and Polydorus. A Romance; translated from the French of the Abbé Barthélemy, Author of the Travels of Anacharsis*. London: Dilly, 1799; rptd. Dublin: Colbert, 1799 [British Museum].

BASTIDE, JEAN FRANÇOIS

*Les Aventures de Victoire Ponty. Amsterdam et Paris, 1758: *Mutual Attachment; or the Memoirs of Victoria de Ponty. A Novel. Translated from the French.* London: Lane, 1784 [Blakey].

BEAURIEU, GASPARD GUILLARD DE, 1728–1795

*L'Elève de la nature. La Haye et Paris, 1763: *The Man of Nature. Translated from the French by James Burne.* 2 vols. London: Cadell, 1773; *"The Officious Friend, a Tale. From *The Man of Nature*, a Work Lately Translated from the French," *Universal*, LII (January-February 1773) [a portion of Burne's translation].

BENOIT, FRANÇOISE ALBINE, b. 1724

*Les Aveux d'une jolie femme. 2 vols. Paris, 1762; 2nd ed., 1782: *Aspasia; or, The Dangers of Vanity. A French Story, taken from real life.* 2 vols. London: Bew, 1791.

BERNARD, CATHERINE, 1662–1712

*Inès de Cordoue. Paris, 1696: "The Unfortunate Lovers, an Historical Anecdote (From Mrs. Thicknesse's *Sketches of the Lives and Writings of the Ladies of France*)," *Universal*, LXIX (November 1781); also "The Following Very Interesting and No Less Entertaining Spanish Tale, Founded on Facts, Is Taken from the *Sketches of the Lives and Writings of the Ladies of France* by Mrs. Thicknesse, Just Published," *London*, L (November-December 1781); also "A Spanish Story. The Following . . . ," *Edinburgh Weekly*, LIV (December 1781)–LV (January 1782); also "The Unfortunate Lovers . . . [same title as the *Universal's*]," *Hibernian Magazine* (December-Appendix 1781); likewise *Westminster*, IX (Supplement 1781); likewise *Weekly Miscellany* (Sherborne), XVII (February-March 1782); also "The Unfortunate Lovers," *Lady's*, XX (August-Supplement 1789); also "Ines de Cordova and the Marquis de Lerma," *Britannic*, VII, No. 98 (1800).

BILLARDON DE SAUVIGNY, EDME LOUIS, 1736–1812

*Histoire amoureuse de Pierre Le Long, Et de sa très honorée Dame Blanche Bazu. Ecritte par iceluy. Londres, 1765: *An Amorous Tale of the Chaste Loves of Peter the Long, and of His Most Honoured Dame Blanche Bazu, His Feal Friend Blaise Bazu, and The History of the Lovers' Well. Imitated from the Original French by Thomas Holcroft.* London: Robinson, 1786.

BITAUBE, Paul Jeremie, 1732–1808

*Joseph, poem en 9 livres (et en prose). Paris, 1757: *Joseph. A Poem [sic]. In Nine Books. Translated from the French of M. Bitaubé [by Kenneth Ferguson]. 2 vols. London: Cadell, 1783.

BONNEVILLE, Nicolas de, 1760–1828

*"Albertine" [translated from the German of Wall], Choix de petits romans, imité de l'allemand. Paris, 1786: "Albertina. An Anecdote Extracted from the Secret History of the Court of ——," Town and Country, XVIII (October 1786)–XIX (January 1787) [translated, according to a note, from both the French and the German, in "An attempt . . . to adapt it to the taste of the English reader"]; likewise Hibernian Magazine (December 1786-February 1787); also "Albertina. From the Secret History of the Court of ——," Edinburgh (2), IV (December 1786); also "Albertina, a Tale, from the German," Universal, LXXXV (July-August 1789); likewise Weekly Entertainer, XIV (September-October 1789).
*"Le Sultan Massoud," Choix de petits romans. Paris, 1786: "Massoud, A Tale, from the French," Edinburgh (2), V (February 1787); likewise Gentleman's and London (Dublin) (May-June 1787).

BRICAIRE DE LA DIXMERIE, Nicolas, d. 1791

*"Abbas et Sohry, nouvelle persane," Contes philosophiques et moraux, par M. de la Dixmérie. Paris, 1765: "Abbas and Sohry, a Persian Tale," Lady's, I (January 1771); likewise Edinburgh (2), IX (February 1789) [but a different translation from the preceding].
*"Azakia, anecdote huronne," Contes philosophiques. Paris, 1765: *"Azakia: a Canadian Story," Universal, XL (April 1767); likewise Universal, LXXIII (February 1783).
*"Cléomir et Dalia, nouvelle gauloise," Contes philosophiques. Paris, 1765: "Cleomir and Dalia. From the Celtic," Lady's, III (January 1772); also "Cleomar and Dalia. A Novel, from the French," Selector (I), Nos. 2–3 (1776).
*"L'Etonnement réciproque, nouvelle orientale," Contes philosophiques. Paris, 1765: *"The Mutual Astonishment, an Oriental Novel, Translated from the French," Universal, XL (January 1767); also "Mutual Astonishment, an Oriental Tale," Lady's, I (January 1771) [a different translation]; also "The Mutual Astonishment, an Oriental Novel," Selector (I), No. 3 (1776) [a third translation,

very short]; also "Mutual Astonishment, an Oriental Tale," *Bath and Bristol*, I, Nos. 10–12 (1782); likewise *New Lady's*, III (February-March 1788); also "The Mutual Astonishment, an Oriental Novel," *New Town and Country*, II (June-July 1788) [*Universal's* translation]; also "The Mutual Surprize, an Oriental Tale," *Lady's*, XXVI (March, May 1795).

*"Giaffar et Abassah, trait d'histoire arabe," *Contes philosophiques*. Paris, 1765: *"Giaffar and Abassah, An Arabian Historical Tract, and Subject for a Tragedy; translated from the French," *Universal*, XL (March 1767).

*"Héraclite et Démocrite, voyageurs," *Contes philosophiques*. Paris, 1765: *"The Travels of Heraclitus and Democritus, Translated from the French, by a Lady," *Lady's*, IV (December-Supplement 1773).

*"L'Oracle journalier," *Contes philosophiques*. Paris, 1765: "The Oracle, an Oriental Tale," *Universal*, XL (February 1767); likewise *New Town and Country*, II (January-February 1788); likewise *Weekly Miscellany* (Glasgow), n.s. II (January-February 1793).

*"Les Solitaires des Pyrénées, nouvelle espagnole et françoise," *Contes philosophiques*. Paris, 1765: "The Pyrenean Hermits," *Lady's*, I (March-April 1771); also "The Pyrenean Hermits, or The Double Discovery. Translated from the French," *New Lady's*, I (February-March 1786); also "The Pyrenean Hermits, A Tale. By M. Dixmerie," *Edinburgh* (2), VIII (December 1788); likewise *Hibernian Magazine* (February-April 1789).

*"Tous Deux se trompoient," *Contes philosophiques*. Paris, 1765: *"The Double Mistake. A Tale, from the French," *Gentleman's*, XXXVI (September-November 1766).

CARRA, JEAN LOUIS, 1743–1793

Odazir, ou le jeune Syrien. Roman philosophique, composé d'après les mémoires d'un Turc. Par M. ***. La Haye, 1772: *Cecilia: or the Eastern Lovers. A Novel. Translated from the French. London: Printed for the author, 1773.

CHARRIERE, ISABELLA AGNETA DE, d. 1805

Lettres écrites de Lausanne. 2 vols. Genève et Paris, 1788: *Letters Written from Lausanne. Translated from the French. 2 vols. Bath, 1799.

CONSTANT DE REBECQUE, SAMUEL DE

*Laure, ou Lettres de quelques femmes de Suisse. 4 vols. Genève et Paris, 1786: Laura, or Letters from Switzerland. By the author of Camille. Translated from the French [by J. Seymour]. 4 vols. London: Hookham, 1788 [Monthly].

CONTANT D'ORVILLE, GUILLAUME, 1730?–1800

—— [French original unidentified]: Pauline; or, The Victim of the Heart. From the French of d'Orville. 2 vols. London: Lane, 1794 [Blakey].

CUBIERES, MICHEL DE, known as Cubières-Palmézeaux, 1752–1820

*Misogug, ou les femmes comme elles sont. Histoire orientale, traduite du chaldéan. Paris, 1787: *Misogug; or, Women as they are. A Chaldean Tale. Translated from the French. 2 vols. London: Elliott, 1788; *"The Good Sovereign: An Oriental Character," Universal, LXXXIII (Supplement 1788) [an unacknowledged extract containing the recital of Misogug's acts of benevolence as a ruler].

DAUBENTON, Mme MARGUERITE

*Zélie dans le désert. 2 vols. Londres et Paris, 1786–87: *Zelia in the Desert. From the French. By the Lady who Translated "Adelaide and Theodore"; and "Anecdotes of Henry IV of France." 3 vols. London: Wilkie, 1789; Zelia in the Desert; or, the Female Crusoe, extracted from the French. London: Forster, 1789 [Analytical].

DORAT, CLAUDE JOSEPH, 1734–1780

*Les Malheurs de l'inconstance, ou lettres de la marquise de Syrcé et du comte de Mirbelle. Amsterdam et Paris, 1772: The Fatal Effects of Inconstancy; or, Letters of the Marchioness de Syrcé, the Count de Mirbelle, and Others. Translated from the French [by Elizabeth Griffith]. 2 vols. London: Bew, 1774 [Block]; *2nd ed., 1777.

DUBOIS-FONTANELLE, JEAN GASPARD, 1737–1812

*Les Effets des passions, ou mémoires de M. de Floricourt. 3 vols. Paris, 1768: *The Effects of the Passions, or Memoirs of Floricourt. From the French. 3 vols. London: Vernor, 1788.
*Naufrage et aventures de M. Pierre Viaud, Natif de Rochefort, Capi-

taine de navire. Bordeaux et Paris, 1768: *The Shipwreck and Adventures of Monsieur Pierre Viaud, A Native of Bordeaux, and Captain of a Ship. Translated from the French, By Mrs.* [Elizabeth] Griffith. London: Davies, 1771; *The True and Surprising adventures, voyages, shipwreck and distresses of Mons. Pierre Viaud, A Native of Bordeaux and Captain of a Ship. Translated by Mrs. Griffiths* [sic]. London: Fisher, 1800 [New York Public Library]; "The Shipwreck and Adventures of Mons. Pierre Viaud. Translated from the French," *Literary Register,* III, Nos. 30–32 (1771) [an abridgement of Mrs. Griffith's translation]; also "The Shipwreck and Adventures of Mon. Pierre Viaud, Translated from the French by Mrs. Griffiths [sic], Who has Favoured the World with *The School for Rakes,* and Many Other Approved Performances," *London,* XL (April-May 1771); likewise *Ipswich,* I (November 1799-February 1800).

DUCLOS, CHARLES PINOT, 1704–1772

Les Confessions du comte de ***, histoire galante. Amsterdam, 1742: *The Pleasures of Retirement, Preferable to the Joys of Dissipation; Exemplified in the Life and Adventures of the Count de B——, Written by Himself. In Letters to a Friend. Now first translated from the original French, by a Lady.* London: Wilkie, 1774 [in fact, a reprint of a 1742 translation]; *A Course of Gallantries; or, the inferiority of the tumultuous joys of the passions to the serene pleasures of reason: attested by the confession of a nobleman who had tried both. Translated from the French of M. Du Clos.* 2 vols. London: Vandenbergh, 1775.

DUCRAY-DUMINIL, FRANÇOIS GUILLAUME, 1761–1819

Alexis, ou la maisonette dans les bois; manuscrit trouvé sur les bords de l'Isère et publié par l'auteur de Lolotte et Fanfan. 4 vols. Grenoble et Paris, 1789: *"Alexis, or the Cottage in the Woods. An Original Novel, from the French," Lady's,* XXII (March 1791)–XXIV (July 1793); likewise *Hibernian Magazine* (April 1791–September 1793).

DUPIN

—— [French original unidentified]: *"Maria Melvil; an Historical Novel. [From the French of the abbé Dupin],"* *Universal,* LXXXV (November 1789).

ELIE DE BEAUMONT, Mme ANNE LOUISE, 1729–1783

Lettres du Marquis de Roselle, par Mme E. de B. Londres et Paris, 1764: *The History of the Marquis de Roselle. In a Series of Letters. By Madam Elie de Beaumont. Translated from the French.* 2 vols. London: Becket and De Hondt, 1765; *The Second Edition, Corrected.* 1766; *"Account of the Letters of the Marquis de Roselle, lately published in France," Gentleman's, XXXV (March 1765).

FAUQUES, MARIANNE AGNES PILLEMENT, *dame* DE, *afterwards Mme Fauques de Vaucluse,* d. 1773

Les Transmigrations d'Hermès [n.p., n.d.; Séguin]: *The Transmigrations of Hermes, a Roman Philosopher, in four volumes. By Madam de ***, The Author of Abassai.* London: Elmsley, 1768 [*Monthly*]; "The Transmigrations of Hermes, a Philosophical Romance. From the French of Madame de Vaucluse. By an English Lady," *Lady's*, V (January-August 1774).

*Le Triomphe de l'amitié, ouvrage traduit du grec, par Mlle de ***.* 2 vols. Londres et Paris, 1751: *"The History of Mirril, a Grecian Tale, Translated from the *Triomphe de l'Amitié," Oxford Magazine*, I (December-Supplement 1768) [an interpolated story from Vol. I].

FIEVEE, JOSEPH, 1767–1839

La Dot de Suzette, ou histoire de Mme de Senneterre, racontée par elle-même. Paris, An VI [1798]: *Suzette's Dowry; or the History of Madam de Senneterre. Related by Herself. Translated from the French.* London, 1799.

FLORIAN, JEAN PIERRE CLARIS DE, 1755–1794

"Bathmendi, nouvelle persane," Les Six Nouvelles de M. de Florian. Paris, 1784: *"Bathmendi: A Persian Tale," Universal*, LXXVIII (February 1786) [an original translation]; likewise *Edinburgh* (2), XIII (January 1791); also "Bathmendi, or the Search after Happiness, a Tale. By M. de Florian," *Lady's*, XXVIII (January-February 1797) [from *Tales, Romances, etc.*; see ANTHOLOGIES].

"Camiré, nouvelle américaine," Nouvelles nouvelles. Paris, 1792: "Camira, an American Tale," *Monthly Extracts*, IV (September 1792) [a review with much quotation].

"Célestine, nouvelle espagnole," Les Six Nouvelles. Paris, 1784:

*"The Adventures of Alphonso and Marina; an interesting Spanish Tale," *Universal*, LXXX (June-Supplement 1787); likewise *Hibernian Magazine* (September-October 1787); also "The Constant Lovers, or the Adventures of Pedro and Celestin [sic]. A Tale. By the Chevalier de Florian," *Edinburgh* (2), XIII (May 1791) [from *Tales, Romances, etc.*; see ANTHOLOGIES]; likewise *Lady's*, XXII (September 1791); likewise *Hibernian Magazine* (October 1791); likewise *Aberdeen* (I), IV (October 1791).

*"Claudine, nouvelle savoyarde," *Nouvelles nouvelles.* Paris, 1792: "Claudina, a Savoyard Tale," *Monthly Extracts*, IV (September 1792) [a review, with extracts, of *New Tales*]; likewise *Edinburgh* (2), XVI (September 1792); likewise *General Magazine*, VI (1792); also "New Tales, from the French of M. Florian," *Universal Magazine and Review*, VIII (December 1792); also "Claudine, A Swiss Tale. From the French of M. de Florian," *European*, XXII (August-September 1792) [this and the following are original translations]; also "Claudine, a Charming Swiss Tale. From the French of the Celebrated M. de Florian," *Bon Ton*, II (August-September 1792); also "Claudine, a Swiss Tale. (From the French of M. de Florian.)," *Scots Magazine*, LIV (September-October 1792); likewise *Sentimental and Masonic*, I (September-October 1792); likewise *Lady's*, XXIII (October-November 1792); likewise *Hibernian Magazine* (October-November 1792).

Estelle, roman pastoral, par M. de Florian. Paris, 1788: *Stella. A pastoral romance. Translated from the French of Mon. de Florian. By Miss Elizabeth Morgan, authoress of Numa Pompilius.* 2 vols. London: Printed and sold for the authoress, 1791; *Estelle by M. de Florian, author of Numa Pompilius, etc. With an essay upon Pastoral. Translated from the French, by Mrs. Susanna Cummyng.* 2 vols. London: Printed for the translator, 1798.

Galatée: roman pastoral imité de Cervantes. Paris, 1783 [British Museum]: *Galatea: a pastoral romance, imitated from Cervantes. Translated by an officer.* Dublin, 1791 [British Museum].

Gonsalve de Cordoue, ou Grenade reconquise, par M. de Florian. Paris, 1791: *Gonsalva of Cordova, or Grenada reconquered. An historical Romance from the French of Florian.* 3 vols. London: Johnson, 1792 [*Analytical*]; *Gonzalva of Cordova or Grenada reconquered, now first translated from the French.* 3 vols. 1793 [Block]; *"Gonzalo de Cordova, or Granada Recovered. An Heroic Romance. (Translated from the French of M. de Florian, Author of *Numa Pompilius, Tales,* etc.)," *Lady's,* XXIII (May 1792)–XXV (June 1795).

—— [French original unidentified]: *"Leucadea, A Spanish Tale, translated from the French of M. de Florian," *Universal,* XCV (October 1794).

Nouvelles nouvelles. Paris, 1792: *New Tales. From the French of M. Florian.* London: Egerton, 1792 [includes "Seymour, an English Tale," "Selico, an African tale," "Claudina, a Savoyard tale," "Zulbar, an Indian tale," "Camira, an American tale," and "Valeria, an Italian tale"].

Numa Pompilius, second roi de Rome. Par M. de Florian, capitaine des dragons et gentilhomme de S.A.S Mgr. le duc de Penthièvre; de l'Académie de Madrid, etc. Paris, 1786: *The History of Numa Pompilius, Second King of Rome. Translated from the French of Mon. de Florian by Miss Elizabeth Morgan.* 2 vols. London: printed for the translator, 1787; *rptd. 1788; *The Adventures of Numa Pompilius of Rome. Translated from the French of M. de Florian.* 2 vols. London: Dilly, 1787 [a different translation]; *rptd. Brussels, 1790 [with French text on facing pages]; *2nd ed., 1798; "Account of Numa Pompilius, Second King of Rome. Translated from the French of M. de Florian, by a Lady," *Town and Country,* XXII (April 1791)–XXIII (October 1793).

Oeuvres de M. de Florian. Paris, 178?: *Works of Chevalier de Florian; containing Galatea, A Pastoral Romance, and other Characteristic Romances. Translated from the last Paris Edition by Mr. Robinson. To which is prefixed an Essay on Pastoral Romance by the Translator.* 2 vols. 1786 [contains *Galatea* and the stories from *Les Six Nouvelles*].

—— [French original unidentified]: *Pieces from M. de Florian* [translated by Joseph Fletcher]. London, 1795 [British Museum].

*"Sélico, nouvelle africaine," *Nouvelles nouvelles.* Paris, 1792: *"Selico, a tale. Translated from the French of M. Florian," *Bee,* X (August 1792); also *"Selico, an African Tale; from New Tales from the French of M. de Florian," *Universal,* XCI (September 1792); also *"Selico, an African Tale; from the French of M. de Florian," *Sentimental and Masonic,* I (October 1792); likewise *Lady's,* XXIII (1792); likewise *Weekly Entertainer* (1793).

*"Sophronime, nouvelle grecque," *Les Six Nouvelles.* Paris, 1784: *"Sophronius; A Grecian Tale," *Universal,* LXXVIII (June 1786).

*"Valérie, nouvelle italienne," *Nouvelles nouvelles.* Paris, 1792:

"Valeria, an Italian Tale," *Edinburgh* (2), XVI (December 1792);
also "Valeria," *General*, LI (1792).

*"Zulbar, nouvelle indienne," *Nouvelles nouvelles*. Paris, 1792: *"Zulbar, an Indian Tale. By M. Florian," *Universal*, XCI (October 1792); likewise *Universal Magazine and Review* (1792); likewise *Sentimental and Masonic*, I (November 1792); likewise *Weekly Entertainer* (1793).

FONTANIEU, Gaspar Moise Augustin de

—— [French original unidentified]: *The Friend of Virtue, or Memoirs of d'Argincourt. A novel. From the French. By the Translator of the Effects of the Passions*. 3 vols. London: Vernor, 1789 [Block].

FOURGUEUX, de

Zély, ou la difficulté d'être heureux, roman indien. Amsterdam et Paris, 1775: *"Zely, or the Difficulty of Being Happy, An Indian Romance," *Sentimental Magazine*, V (June-July 1777); likewise *Monthly Miscellany*, V (June-July 1777); likewise *Gentleman's and London* (Dublin) (July-August 1777).

FRAMERY, Nicolas Etienne, 1745–1810

Mémoires de M. le Marquis de S. Forlaix, recueillis dans les lettres de sa famille, par M. Framéry. 4 vols. Paris, 1770: *Memoirs of the Marquis de St. Forlaix, Translated from the French, of Mons. Framery. By Mrs. Brooke*. 4 vols. London: Dodsley, 1770.

GAYOT DE PITAVAL, François, 1673–1743

Causes célèbres et intéressantes, avec les jugemens qui les ont décidées. Paris, 1735–45 [Library of Congress]: *The Romance of Real Life, by Charlotte Smith*. 3 vols. London: Cadell, 1787 [New York Public Library].

"Jacques LeBrun," *Causes célèbres*. Paris, 1735–45: "The History of James Le Brun (From *The Romances of Real Life*, by Charlotte Smith)," *Political*, XIV (January-February 1788); likewise *Hibernian Magazine* (February, May 1788).

"Martin Guerre," *Causes célèbres*. Paris, 1735–45: "The Pretended Martin Guerre. Extracted from the *Causes Celebres*. By Miss C[harlotte] Smith," *Edinburgh* (2), VI (August 1787); likewise *Caledonian* (I), I (September-October 1787); also "The Pretended Martin Guerre. An Authentic History," *Weekly Miscellany* (Glasgow), III, Nos. 74–76 (November-December 1790).

GENLIS, STEPHANIE FELICITE, *comtesse* DE
afterwards marquise de Sillery, 1746–1830
*Adèle et Théodore, ou Lettres sur l'éducation. 3 vols. Paris, 1782:
**Adelaide and Theodore, or Letters on education. Translated from
the French of Madame la comtesse de Genlis.* 3 vols. London: Bathurst and Cadell, 1783; *2nd ed., corrected and emended.* 1784
[British Museum]; 3rd ed., 1788 [Bibliothèque Nationale]; 4th
ed. London: Cadell and Davis, 1796 [NCBEL]; *"Adela and
Theodore, or Letters on Education. Translation of an excellent little
work just published at *Paris,* intitled *Adela et Theodore, ou Lettres sur l'education,*" *Universal,* LXX (June 1782)–LXXIX (December 1786); also "Adelaide and Theodore, or Letters on Education. Containing All the Principles Relating to Three Different
Plans of Education for Princes, Young Ladies, and Young Gentlemen," *Lady's,* XVI (May 1785)–XX (April 1789) [another
translation, uncompleted].
———: **The Beauties of Genlis; being a select collection, of the most
beautiful tales and other striking extracts, from Adela and Theodore; The Tales of the Castle; The Theatre of Education and Sacred Dramas; written by the Countess de Genlis.* Perth, 1787
[contains, among other works, "The History of Cecilia, the Beautiful Nun," "The Brazier; or, Reciprocal Gratitude," "The History
of the Dutchess of C———," "The Solitary Family of Normandy,"
"The History of Saint Andre," "The Castle of Truth, a moral tale,"
and "Eglantine; or, Indolence Reformed"]; 2nd ed. Perth, 1788
[British Museum]; 3rd ed. Dublin, 1791 [*Analytical*].
**Les Chevaliers du cygne, ou la cour de Charlemagne. Conte historique et moral pour servir de suite aux Veillées du Château, et
dont tous les traits qui peuvent faire allusion à la révolution françoise sont tirés de l'Histoire. Par Mme de Genlis.* 3 vols. Hambourg,
1795: **The Knights of the Swan; or, the Court of Charlemagne: a
historical and moral tale: to serve as a continuation to The Tales
of the Castle: and of which all the incidents that bear analogy to
the French Revolution are taken from history. Translated from
the French of Madame de Genlis by the Rev. M. Beresford.* 3 vols.
London: Johnson, 1796; rptd. Dublin, 1797 [New York Public
Library]; *The Age of Chivalry; or, Friendship of other Times: a*

moral and historical tale, abridged and selected from the Knights of the Swan, by Madame de Genlis, by C. Butler. London: Peacock, 1799 [Block].

"Daphnis et Pandrose, ou les Oréades," *Les Veillées du château.* Paris, 1784: "Daphnis and Pandrose, a Moral Tale," *New Lady's,* VII (June-October 1792).

"Histoire de la Duchesse de C***, écrite par elle-même," *Adèle et Théodore.* Vol. I. Paris, 1782: "Female Fortitude, or the History of the Duchess of C——, Written by Herself," *Lady's,* XVII (January-July 1786) [unacknowledged as by Mme de Genlis, and enough removed from the portion of *Adelaide and Theodore* currently being serialized by the *Lady's* that the duplication was not observed].

"Histoire de M. de la Palinière," *Les Veillées du château.* Vol. I. Paris, 1782: *"The Fatal Effects of Indulging the Passions: Exemplified in the History of M. de la Paliniere. By Madame Genlis," *European,* VI (December 1784)–VII (February 1785) [identical to, and probably an early printing of, Holcroft's translation]; likewise *Hibernian Magazine* (January-May 1785); also "The Slave of Sensuality, or Fatal Effects of Indulging the Passions. A Moral Story. From the French of Madame Genlis," *New Novelist's,* II (1787).

"Histoire de St. André," *Adèle et Théodore.* Vol. II. Paris, 1782: "Affecting History of St. Andre. (By the Countess de Genlis)," *Weekly Miscellany* (Glasgow), IV, Nos. 95–99 (April-May 1791) [reprint from the *Universal's* translation of *Adela and Theodore*].

**Les Mères rivales, ou la calomnie, Par madame de Genlis.* 3 vols. Paris, An IX [1800]: **The Rival Mothers, or Calumny. Translated from the French of Madame de Genlis.* 4 vols. London: Longman and Rees, 1800.

**Les Veillées du château, ou cours de morale à l'usage des enfans; par l'auteur d'Adèle et Théodore.* 3 vols. Paris, 1782: **Tales of the Castle: Or, Stories of Instruction and Delight. Being Les Veillées du Chateau, written in French by Madame la Comtesse de Genlis. Author of The Theatre of Education, Adela and Theodore, etc. Translated into English by Thomas Holcroft.* 5 vols. London: Robinson, 1785 [the stories in Vol. V of Holcroft's translation are not found in the French original]; rptd. Dublin, 1785 [NCBEL]; 3rd ed., 1787 [NCBEL]; 5th ed., 1798 [New York Public Library].

**Les Voeux téméraires, ou l'Enthousiasme. Par Madame de Genlis.* 3 vols. Hambourg, 1799: **Rash Vows, or, The Effects of Enthusiasm.*

A Novel. Translated from the French of Madame de Genlis. 3 vols. London: Longman and Rees, 1799; rptd. Dublin, 1799 [NCBEL].

GORJY, JEAN CLAUDE, 1753–1795

Blançay, par l'auteur du Nouveau voyage sentimental. 2 vols. Londres et Paris, 1788: *Blansay. A tale of incidents in life. From the French. By the author of Victorina, Louis and Nina, etc.* 2 vols. London: Lane, 1790 [Blakey].

Lidorie, ancienne chronique allusive, publiée par l'auteur de Blançay. 2 vols. Paris, 1790: *Lidora; an Ancient Chronicle. From the French of Mon. de Gorgy, author of Blansay, Victorina, and St. Alma.* 2 vols. London: Lane, 1791.

Nouveau voyage sentimental. Paris, 1785: *Louis and Nina; or, An Excursion to Yverdun.* 2 vols. London: Lane, 1787 [Blakey].

Saint Alme, par l'auteur de Blançay, etc. 2 vols. Paris, 1790 [Monglond]: *St. Alma. A Novel. Translated from the French of J.C. Gorgy, by Mrs. Helme.* 2 vols. London: Lane, 1791 [Blakey].

Tablettes sentimentales du bon Pamphile, Pendant les mois d'Août, Septembre, Octobre et Novembre, en 1789. Publiées par M. Gorjy. Paris, 1791: *Sentimental Tablets of the Good Pamphile, written in the months of August, September, October, and November, 1789, by M. Gorjy. Translated from the French by P.S. Dupuy of the East-India House.* London: Printed at the Philanthropic Reform, 1795 [Block gives Charles Lamb partial credit for this translation].

Victorine, par l'auteur de Blançay, etc. 2 vols. Paris, 1789: *Victorina. An interesting and incidental tale. By the Author of Blansay, Louis and Nina, etc. Translated from the French.* 2 vols. London: Lane, 1790.

GRAFFIGNY, FRANÇOISE D'ISSEMBOURG D'HAPPONCOURT DE, 1695–1758

Lettres d'une Péruvienne. A Peine, s.d. [1747; edition of 1749 includes the anonymous "Suite des *Lettres péruviennes*"; the edition of 1763 includes the "Suite" and Lamarche-Courmont's *Lettres d'Aza ou d'un Péruvien*]: *Letters written by a Peruvian Princess. Translated from the French.* London: Cooper, 1768 [contents those of the 1747 French edition; this work had already appeared in 1748 and 1752, according to NCBEL]; *Letters written by a Peruvian Princess. Translated from the French. A new edition, in two volumes.* London: Robinson, 1771 [includes both the "Suite" and the *Lettres d'Aza*]; *The Peruvian Letters, Translated from the*

French. With an additional original Volume. By R. Roberts, Translator of Select Tales from Marmontel, Author of Sermons by a Lady, and Translator of the History of France, from the abbé Millot. 2 vols. London: Cadell, 1774; *Letters written by a Peruvian Princess. Translated from the French* [by Francis Ashmore]. 2 vols. 1782 [NCBEL; includes "Suite" and *Lettres d'Aza*]; rptd. 1787 [NCBEL]; rptd. 1795 [NCBEL]; rptd. 1796 [NCBEL]; "Letter from a Peruvian Princess to her Lover, Giving an Account of Her Being Taken out of the Temple of the Sun by the Spaniards," *Weekly Amusement,* II (July 1765)–III (September 1766) [includes only those letters by Mme de Graffigny]; also **"Letters of a Peruvian Princess, with the Sequel. Translated from the French of Madame de Graffigny, by Francis Ashmore, Esq. In Two Volumes," Novelist's Magazine,* IX (1782).

HELVETIUS, CLAUDE ADRIEN, 1715–1771

—— [French original nonexistent]: **The Child of Nature, Improved by Chance. A Philosophical Novel by Mr. Helvetius.* 2 vols. London: Becket, 1774; **The Philosophy of Pleasure; Or, the History of a Young Lady, Of Luxurious Temperament and Prurient Imagination, who experiences repeatedly the Dangers of Seduction and whose escapes from the Snares of Love are truly wonderful, depicting many and various Luscious Scenes with her Lovers, and proving herself to be the Child of Nature Improved by Chance. Freely translated from the original French.* London: Becket, 1774 [same work as the preceding; the forward ascribes it to Helvétius, an attribution which is of course false]; ***"The Child of Nature improved by Chance; a Philosophical Novel, by Mr. Helvetius," *Universal,* LIV (Supplement 1774) [an extract from the beginning of the novel].

IMBERT, BARTHELEMI, 1747–1790

*"Rosette" [published in the *Mercure de France*]: "Rosetta, a Tale, by M. Imbert," *Lady's,* XXII (November-December 1791).

LAMARCHE-COURMONT, IGNACE HUGARY DE

*Lettres d'Aza, ou d'un Péruvien. Conclusion des Lettres Péruviennes. Amsterdam, 1749: "Letters of Aza. Translated by the Author of *The Old English Baron* [Clara Reeve]," *Lady's,* IX (June-July 1778); X (July 1779)–XI (February 1780) [only the first two letters were translated by Clara Reeve, the rest being done by "D"

after she abandoned the project; see Mayo, pp. 312–317, for a discussion of the affair]; also "The Sequel of the Peruvian Princess, Containing the Letters of Aza," *Novelist's Magazine*, IX (1782) [appended to Ashmore's translation of Mme de Graffigny's letters]; also "Letters of Aza," *Smith's Weekly*, I, No. 4 (February 1793–?) [for further reprints, see GRAFFIGNY].

LA MOTTE

"Salned et Garaldi," *Mercure de France* (October 1751): "The False Appearances, or Innocence Vindicated. A Persian Tale," *Every Man's*, I (March-April 1772).

LA SALLE, ADRIEN NICOLAS, marquis DE

*Histoire de Sophie de Francourt. Par Monsieur de ***.* 2 vols. Paris, 1768: *Integrity, or the History of Sophia Francourt, from the French.* 2 vols. London: Beilby, 1790 [Block].

LAVALLEE, JOSEPH, marquis de Bois-Robert, 1747–1816

Cécile, fille d'Achmet III, Empereur des Turcs, née en 1710. 2 vols. Constantinople et Paris, 1787: *Maria Cecilia; or Life and Adventures of the Daughter of Achmet III, Emperor of the Turks. From the French.* 2 vols. London: Lane, 1788.

Le Nègre, comme il y a peu de blancs. Par l'auteur de Cécile, fille d'Achmet III, Empereur des Turcs. 3 vols. Madras et Paris, 1789: *The Negro as there are few white men. Translated from the French, by J. Trapp.* 3 vols. London: The author, 1790 [Library of Congress]; *The Negro, Equalled by Few Europeans. Translated from the French.* 3 vols. London: Robinson, 1790 [*Analytical*]; *"The Negro, Equalled by Few Europeans. An Extract from a Beautiful Novel of That Name Just Published in Three Volumes by Messrs Robinsons. Containing the False Imprisonment of Itanoko (the Negro), His Examination before the Judges, and Other Matters," Lady's*, XXI (June-September 1790); likewise *Hibernian Magazine* (August-November 1790).

LEONARD, NICOLAS GERMAIN, 1744–1793

Lettres de deux amans, habitans de Lyon. Publiées par M. Léonard. 3 vols. Londres et Paris, 1783: *The Correspondence of Two Lovers, Inhabitants of Lyons. Published from the French Originals.* 3 vols. London: Hookham, and Robinson, 1788 [Block].

LE PRINCE DE BEAUMONT, MARIE, 1711–1780

*Contes moraux. Par Madame Le Prince de Beaumont. 2 vols. Lyon et Paris, 1774: *Moral Tales. Translated from the French of Mde Le Prince de Beaumont. 2 vols. London: Nourse, 1775 [this translation includes the following: Vol. I, "The Judge of her own Failing" ("Le Juge de sa propre faute"), "The History of Celestia" ("Histoire de Céleste"), "The True Point of Honour, a Moral History" ("Le Vrai Point d'honneur"); Vol. II, "The True Point of Honour, concluded"].

*"Histoire de Céleste," Contes moraux. Vol. I. Paris, 1774: *The Fatal Indifference; or, the interesting history of Mrs. Matilda Markham. To which is added, The History of Celestia, (translated from the French). London: Bassan, 1800 [?]; *"History of Celestia. From the French," Lady's, VIII (June-July 1777).

*"Le Juge de sa propre faute," Contes moraux. Vol. I. Paris, 1774: *"Olympia, or the Acquisitions of Experience. Translated from the French, by a Lady," Lady's, VII (December 1776)–VIII (June 1777).

*Lettres de Madame du Montier à la marquise de ***, sa fille, avec les réponses. Lyon, 1758; modified in the Lyon 1767 edition and called Lettres de Madame du Montier, recueillies par Mme Le Prince de Beaumont: *Letters of Madame du Montier, collected by Madame Le Prince de Beaumont. Translated from the French, by Miss Newman, in 3 vols. London: Hookham and Carpenter, 1797.

*Lettres d'Emérance à Lucie. Par Mad^{me} Le Prince de Beaumont. Lyon, 1765: *Letters from Emerance to Lucy. Translated from the French of Madame Le Prince de Beaumont. 2 vols. London: Nourse, 1766.

*Mémoires de madame la baronne de Batteville, ou la veuve parfaite. Par mad^{me} Le Prince de Beaumont. Londres: Nourse, 1766: *The Virtuous Widow; or, Memoirs of the Baroness de Batteville. Translated from the French of Madame Le Prince de Beaumont. Dublin: Williams, 1767.

*La Nouvelle Clarice, histoire véritable. Par Mme Le Prince de Beaumont. Lyon, 1767: *The New Clarissa: A True History. By Madame de Beaumont. 2 vols. London: Nourse, 1768.

*Le Triomphe de la vérité, ou mémoires de Mr. de la Villete. Par Mme Le Prince D.B. 2 vols. Nancy, 1748: The Triumph of Truth; or, Memoirs of Mr. De la Vilette. Translated from the French by R. Roberts. With a Vignette title. 2 vols. London: Cadell, 1775 [Block].

*"Le Vrai Point d'honneur," *Contes moraux*. Vols. I–II. Paris, 1774: *"The True Point of Honour, A Moral History, in a Series of Letters. Translated from the French, by a Lady," *Lady's*, VIII (August 1777)–XI (Supplement 1780).

LOAISEL DE TREOGATE, JOSEPH MARIE, 1752–1812

Le Fils naturel. 2 vols. Genève et Paris, 1789; also issued under the title *Jules et Sophie, ou le fils naturel: Julius; or, The Natural Son. Translated from the French*. 2 vols. London: Ridgeway, 1789 [Summers]; *The Natural Son; A Novel, in two Vols. Translated from the French of M. Diderot, Author of The Nun, James the Fatalist, etc.* London: Longman, 1799 [the attribution to Diderot is false; as the plot summary given in the September 1799 review in the *Monthly* makes clear, this is a translation of *Le Fils naturel*].

LOUVET DE COUVRAI, JEAN BAPTISTE, 1760–1797

Emilie de Varmont, ou le divorce nécessaire, et les amours du curé Sévin, par l'auteur de Faublas. 3 vols. Paris, 1791: *Emily de Varmont; or Divorce Dictated by Necessity; To which are added The Amours of Father Sévin. From the French of Louvet*. 3 vols. London: Kearsley, 1798.
Une Année de la vie du Chevalier de Faublas. 4 vols. Londres et Paris, 1787; further volumes in 1788 and 1790: *Life and Adventures of the Chevalier de Faublas*. 4 vols. London, 1793 [*Monthly*]; *"The Adventures of the Baron de Lovzinski. Extracted from The Life of the Chevalier de Faublas," *Lady's*, XXV (October 1794)– XXVI (April 1795); likewise *Hibernian Magazine* (November 1794-June 1795).

MARMONTEL, JEAN-FRANÇOIS, 1723–1799

*"L'Amitié à l'épreuve," *Contes moraux*. Paris, 1765: "The Trial of Friendship. A Story Now First Translated from the Third Volume of *Contes Moraux*, just published by Marmontel," *Gentleman's*, XXXV (June-July 1765) [first English translation]; likewise *Scots*, XXVII (June-July 1765); also "The Trial of Friendship, a Moral Tale," *Weekly Amusement*, II (November-December 1765); also "Friendship put to the Test. A Moral Tale," *Universal Museum*, n.s. III (November-December 1767); also "Friendship put to the Test. From the French of Marmontel. Translated by a Young Lady," *Lady's*, XII (March-July 1781) [a new translation, signed R——]; likewise *Hibernian Magazine* (April-October

1781); also "The Trial of Friendship, a Moral Tale," *New Universal* (2), I (July-December 1787).

*"Annette et Lubin," *Contes moraux*. Paris, 1765: *"*Anette* and *Lubin*; said to be a true story. From the *French*," *Gentleman's*, XXXI (September 1761); also *"Annete and Lubin: A true Story.— From M. Marmontel's Moral Tales just published," *Universal*, XXXIII (December 1763); also *"Lubin and Annetta. A true story," *Lady's*, VII (July 1776).

*"Les Bateliers de Besons, conte moral," *Nouveaux Contes moraux*. Liège, 1792: "The Waterman of Besons, a Moral Tale," *Universal*, XCII (January-March 1793) [identified in a note as Marmontel's]; also "The Waterman of Besons. By Marmontel," *Sentimental and Masonic*, II (February-April 1793).

Bélisaire. Par M. Marmontel, de l'Académie françoise. Paris, 1767: *Belisarius. By M. Marmontel, member of the French Academy*. London: Vaillant, 1767; *A new translation*. London: Cooper, 1768 [British Museum]; *Belisarius, and Fragments of Moral Philosophy*. 1784 [NCBEL]; rptd. 1786 [NCBEL]; *Translated by F. Ashmore*. London: Harrison, 1789; *rptd. Brussels, 1792 [with French text on facing pages]; *A New Edition*. London: Vernor and Hood, 1794 [British Museum]; rptd. 1796 [NCBEL]; rptd. 1800 [NCBEL]; "Belisarius. By M. Marmontel," *Scots*, XXXIX (April 1767) [a long review, the last 3500 words of which are identical with the *Monthly*'s April critique]; also *"Extract from M. Marmontel's Belisarius, on the Subject of Religion," *London Magazine*, XXXVI (April 1767).

*"La Bergère des Alpes," *Contes moraux*. Paris, 1765: *The Shepherdess of the Alpes; or Virtue's sure reward. Being a very interesting, pathetic and moral tale, founded on facts*. London: Sabine, n.d. [Library of Congress]; *Aglaura. A Tale. Taken from the French in Marmontel's Moral Tales. By Mr.* [Elisha] *Trapaud*. London [?]: Brotherton and Sewell, 1774 [*Critical*]; *The Shepherdess of the Alps, a very interesting, pathetic, and moral tale . . .* London: W. Clements, J. Sadler, and J. Eves, 1792 [McBurney]; *The Shepherdess of the Alps*. 1794 [NCBEL]; *The Shepherdess of the Alps: A Very Interesting, Pathetic, and Moral Tale. Published at the Request of Several Ladies of Distinction*. Manchester: Swindells, ca. 1796–99 [Block]; "The Shepherdess of the Alps, a Moral Tale," *Weekly Amusement*, I (January 1764) [Becket and De Hondt's version]; likewise *Caledonian Weekly*, I (June 1773–?); likewise *Weekly Miscellany* (Sherborne), VIII (June-July

1777); likewise *Moral and Entertaining*, I (July-August 1777); likewise *New London*, VI (December 1790)–VII (April 1791); likewise *New Lady's*, VIII (October 1793), IX (February-August 1794); likewise *Gentleman's and London* (Dublin) (December 1793)—(April-July 1794).

*"La Bonne Mère," *Contes moraux.* Paris, 1765: "The Good Mother, a Moral Tale," *Weekly Amusement*, I (March-April 1764) [Becket and De Hondt's version]; also *"The Daughter taught the Choice of a Husband.—A Moral Tale," *Universal*, XLVIII (January 1771) [unacknowledged as Marmontel's]; also "The Good Mother, a Moral Tale," *Caledonian Weekly*, I (July 1773); likewise *Weekly Miscellany* (Sherborne), X (September 1778)–XI (October 1778); likewise *Moral and Entertaining*, III (October 1778).

*"La Cassette, conte moral," *Nouveaux Contes moraux.* Liège, 1792: "The Casket, a Moral Tale. By Marmontel," *Edinburgh* (2), n.s. II (August-September 1793); also *"Hortensia, or the Wisdom of Explanation. A New Moral Tale, by M. de Marmontel," *Universal*, XCIV (April-May 1794); likewise *Hibernian Magazine* (May-June 1794); also "Hortensia, a Moral Tale," *Scots*, LVI (June-July 1794); also "Hortensia, or the Wisdom of Explanation," *Weekly Entertainer*, XXXIII (June 1799)–XXXIV (July 1799).

*"Le Connoisseur," *Contes moraux.* Paris, 1765: "The Connoisseur. From Marmontel's Tales," *Universal*, XXXIII (Supplement 1763) [Becket and De Hondt's version]; likewise *Weekly Miscellany* (Sherborne), X (September 1778); likewise *Moral and Entertaining*, III (September 1778).

Contes moraux. Par Mr. Marmontel, suivis d'une apologie du Théâtre. 2 vols. Amsterdam, 1761; later augmented and issued as *Contes moraux, par M. Marmontel.* 3 vols. Paris, 1765: **Select Moral Tales. Translated from the French, by a Lady* [R. Roberts]. Glocester: Raikes, 1763 [includes "The Good Mother," "The Shepherdess of the Alps," "The Happy Divorce," and "The Partial Mother"]; *Moral Tales, by M. Marmontel.* 2 vols. London: Becket and De Hondt, 1764. Vol. III added in 1766; *Moral Tales of M. Marmontel.* 2 vols. London: Kearsley, 1764 [translated by Charles Denis and Robert Lloyd; several stories had already appeared in Lloyd's *St. James's Magazine* before the collection was issued]; *Moral Tales, by M. Marmontel.* 3 vols. Edinburgh, 1768 [NCBEL]; rptd. 1781 [NCBEL]; rptd. Manchester, 1790 [?] [NCBEL]; rptd. Dublin, 1792 [New York Public Library]; rptd. 1795 [NCBEL]; *Marmontel's Tales, Selected and abridged, for the Instruction and*

Amusement of Youth. By Mrs. [Mary] *Pilkington.* London: Vernor and Hood, 1799; *Moral Tales, by M. Marmontel.* 3 vols. 1800 [NCBEL]; *"Moral Tales, by M. Marmontel. Translated from the French, by C. Dennis and R. Lloyd. In three volumes," *Novelist's Magazine,* VI (1781) [erroneously attributed to Denis and Lloyd and actually the anonymous translation published by Becket and De Hondt].

*"Les Deux Infortunées," *Contes moraux.* Paris, 1765: "The Two Unfortunate Ladies, a Moral Tale," *Weekly Amusement,* I (October 1764) [Becket and De Hondt's version].

*"L'Ecole des pères," *Contes moraux.* Paris, 1765: "The School for Fathers. A Moral Tale," *St. James's* (I), II (July 1763) [Denis and Lloyd's translation]; also "The School for Fathers. A Moral Tale," *Weekly Amusement,* I (May-June 1764) [same title, but Becket and De Hondt's version].

*"L'Erreur d'un bon père," *Nouveaux Contes moraux.* Liège, 1792: "The Error of a Good Father. A Tale, by M. Marmontel," *Universal,* XC (April-May 1792); likewise *Monthly Extracts,* III (May 1792) [an extract in a review]; likewise *Universal Magazine and Review,* VII (June 1792)–VIII (October 1792); likewise *Weekly Entertainer,* XX (July 1792).

*"La Femme comme il y en a peu," *Contes moraux.* Paris, 1765: "The Good Wife, a Moral Tale," *Court Miscellany,* I (November-December 1765); also "A Wife of Ten Thousand, A Moral Tale," *Weekly Miscellany* (Sherborne), II (September 1774); likewise *Weekly Miscellany* (London), Nos. 106–107 (1774); also "The Extraordinary Wife. From Marmontel. A New Translation. By Louisa D'Argent," *Lady's,* XI (March-May 1780).

*"Le Franc Breton," *Nouveaux Contes moraux.* Liège, 1792: "The Honest Breton," *Monthly Extracts,* II (April 1792).

*"Heureusement," *Contes moraux.* Paris, 1765: "Happily. A Moral Tale," *St. James's* (I), II (June 1763) [identified as Marmontel's]; likewise *Beauties of All the Magazines,* II (July 1763); also "Happily. A Moral Tale, from the French," *New Lady's,* VIII (Supplement 1793)–IX (February 1794); likewise *Hibernian Magazine* (March-April 1794).

*"L'Heureux Divorce," *Contes moraux.* Paris, 1765: "The Happy Divorce. A Moral Tale," *Weekly Amusement,* I (July-September 1764) [Becket and De Hondt's version].

*"Il le fallait," *Nouveaux Contes moraux.* Liège, 1792: "There Was no Help for it. A Moral Tale," *General,* VI (1792).

*_Les Incas, ou La Destruction de l'Empire du Pérou; Par M. Marmontel, Historiographe de France, membre de l'Académie française, etc._ 2 vols. Paris, 1777: *_The Incas: or, The Destruction of the Empire of Peru. By M. Marmontel._ 2 vols. London: Nourse, 1777; *rptd. Dublin, 1777; rptd. Dublin: Stewart, 1797 [Library of Congress]; *Britton, John. _Sheridan and Kotzebue._ London: Fairburn, 1799 [as the lengthy title page states, Britton quotes "The Histories of Alonzo and Cora, On which Kotzebue founded his two celebrated Plays of _The Virgin of the Sun_ and _The Death of Rolla_"]; "Histoire de la ruine de la ville de Mexico, tirée des Incas de M. Marmontel," _Magazin à la mode_, I (October-November 1777); also *"The History of the Incas, or the Destruction of the Empire of Peru. Translated from the French of the Celebrated Mr. Marmontel," _Universal_, LXI (November 1777)–LXII (February 1778) [taken and much abridged from Nourse's publication]; likewise _Westminster_, VI (March-May 1778).

*"Laurette," _Contes moraux._ Paris, 1765: "The History of Lauretta. A Moral Tale," _Court Miscellany_, I (July-October 1765) [first English translation]; also "Lauretta. A Moral Tale," _Weekly Amusement_, III (January-March 1766); also "Lauretta. A New Translation from the French of Marmontelle. By Harriot Delany, a Young Lady of Nineteen," _Lady's_, XI (August-November 1780); also "Lauretta. A Moral Tale," _Thespian_, II (November 1793)–III (April 1794).

*"Lausus et Lydie," _Contes moraux._ Paris, 1765: *"Lausus and Lydia, a Tale. From the Translation of the French of _Marmontel_, Published by _Becket_ and _de Hondt_," _Gentleman's_, XXXIII (December 1763).

*"La Leçon du malheur, conte moral," _Nouveaux Contes moraux._ Liège, 1792: *"The Lesson of Misfortune, a Moral Tale," _Universal_, XC (March 1792); also "The Lesson of Misfortune. From Marmontel," _Gentleman's and London_ (March-May 1792); also "The Lesson of Misfortune, a Moral Tale. From the French of the Celebrated M. Marmontel," _Weekly Entertainer_, XIX (May-June 1792); also "The Lesson of Misfortune," _Monthly Extracts_, III (May 1792); likewise _Universal Magazine and Review_, VII (May-June 1792); likewise _General_, VI (1792); also "A Lesson from Adversity. A Tale, Translated from the French of Marmontel, by a Friend," _Bee_, XIII (January-February 1793) [translated "For the _Bee_"].

*"Le Mari sylphe," _Contes moraux._ Paris, 1765: "The Husband

Turned Sylph. A Tale. Translated from the Third Volume of Marmontel's *Tales*, Lately Published," *British* (2), VI (November-December 1765) [first English translation]; also "The Sylph Husband, a Moral Tale. A New Translation from Marmontel. By Miss Georgiana H———t, a Young Lady between Sixteen and Seventeen," *Lady's*, XI (December 1780)– XII (February 1781).

*"Les Mariages Samnites, anecdote ancienne," *Contes moraux*. Paris, 1765: "The Marriages of the Samnites. An Ancient Anecdote," *St. James's* (I), II (August 1763) [Denis and Lloyd's translation].

*"La Mauvaise Mère," *Contes moraux*. Paris, 1765: "The Bad Mother, a Moral Tale. By the Author of 'The Shepherdess of the Alps,'" *Weekly Amusement*, I (February-March 1764); also *"The Favourite. A Moral Tale," *Universal*, LXVII (Supplement 1770) [unacknowledged as Marmontel's]; also "The Bad Mother, a Moral Tale," *Caledonian Weekly*, I (June 1773–?); also "The Bad Mother, a Moral Tale, by M. Marmontel," *Bristol and Bath*, II, No. 13 (1783).

Nouveaux Contes moraux. 2 vols. Liège, 1792: *The Tales of an Evening, Followed by the Honest Breton. Translated from the French of M. Marmontel. Vol. I. London: Bew, 1792; *Tales. Translated from the French of M. Marmontel. Vol. II. London: Bew, 1792; *New Moral Tales. Now first translated from the French of M. Marmontel. Vol. III. London: Bew, 1793; *New Moral Tales. Now First Translated from the French of M. Marmontel. Vol. IV. London: Bew, 1794; *A New Collection of Moral Tales, Chiefly Written by the Celebrated Marmontel and translated from the original French, by Mr. Heron. 3 vols. Perth: Morison, and London: Lane, 1792 [besides those stories of Marmontel, the collection contains "Lucia and Melania," "The Triumph of Fraternal Friendship," "Emilius and Sophia" from Rousseau's *Emile*, and "Adventures of a Young Woman confined in a Hollow Oak"]; *Tales, translated from the French of M. Marmontel. Consisting of Tales of an Evening, and the Honest Breton. Dublin: Wogan, 1792 [Heron's translation].

*"Le Philosophe soi-disant," *Contes moraux*. Paris, 1765: "The Pretended Philosopher. A Humourous Character, from Marmontel's *Moral Tales*," *Universal Museum*, II (November 1763)–III (January 1764) [a fragment from Becket and De Hondt's version, minus the first 1200 words]; likewise *Weekly Amusement*, II (March-April 1765).

*"Soliman II," *Contes moraux*. Paris, 1765: "Soliman the Second. A Moral Tale," *St. James's* (I), III (September 1763) [Denis and

Lloyd's translation]; likewise *Edinburgh Museum*, I (September 1763); likewise *Beauties of All the Magazines*, II (October 1763); also "Solyman the Second. A Moral Tale," *Dublin* (I), II (October 1763); also "The History of Soliman and Elmira. Translated from the French and Illustrated with a Beautiful Copper-plate," *Court Miscellany*, IV (July-August 1768) [Becket and De Hondt's version]; also "Soliman II, Translated from Marmontel, by a Lady, and Addressed to the Rev. Mr. Madan, and Author of *Thelypthora*," *Lady's*, XII (September, October, Supplement 1781) [another different translation].

*"Les Solitaires de Murcie, conte moral," *Nouveaux Contes moraux*. Liège, 1792: "The Recluses of Murcia. A New Tale by Marmontel," *Carlton House*, I (January-April 1792).

*"Tout ou rien," *Contes moraux*. Paris, 1765: "All or Nothing, a Moral Tale," *Weekly Amusement*, II (January-February 1765) [Becket and De Hondt's version].

*"La Veillée," tales 4 and 5, *Nouveaux Contes moraux*. Liège, 1792: *"The Mill, a Tale," *Universal*, XC (January 1792) and "The Good Vicar, a Sequel to 'The Mill, a Tale,' by M. Marmontel," *ibid.*, XC (February 1792) [two connecting stories]; likewise *Gentleman's and London* (Dublin) (February 1792) and (March 1792); also "The Mill, a Tale, From the French of the Celebrated Marmontel," *Weekly Entertainer*, XIX (February 1792) and "The Good Vicar, a Sequel to 'The Mill, a Tale,' by M. Marmontel," *ibid.*, XX (December 1792).

MASSON DE MORVILLIERS, Nicolas

Adelaide, ou l'amour et le repentir. Paris, 1769 [*Bibliothèque universelle des romans*]: *Adelaide; or, Conjugal Affection. From the French*. London: Lane, 1785 [Blakey; the attribution is due to comments in the November 1785 *Monthly*].

MERCIER, Louis Sebastien, 1740–1814

*"L'Optimisme," *Songes philosophiques. Par M. Mercier*. Londres et Paris, 1768: *"Optimism, a Dream, by M. Mercier," *European*, XI (January-February 1787); likewise *Hibernian Magazine* (February-March 1787); likewise *Weekly Miscellany* (Glasgow), IV, Nos. 92–94 (March-April 1797).

*"Vivonne et Ruyter," *Fictions morales, par M. Mercier*. Paris, 1792: *"Seraphina, a Novel, from the French of M. Mercier," *Lady's*, XXV (August-September 1794).

MONTESQUIEU, CHARLES LOUIS DE SECONDAT,
baron DE LA BREDE et DE, 1689–1755

*"Arsace et Isménie, histoire orientale," Oeuvres posthumes de M. de
Montesquieu. Londres et Paris, 1783: The Temple of Gnidus, and
Arsaces and Ismenia. Translated from the French. London, 1797
[British Museum]; *"Arsaces and Ismena, an Oriental History.
Now first Translated from the Posthumous Works of the Celebrated
Montesquieu," Universal, LXXIV (May-June 1784); likewise
Hibernian Magazine (June-September 1784); also "Arsaces and
Ismena, an Oriental History," Caledonian Magazine and Review,
III (June-August 1784); also "Arsaces and Ismenia, an Oriental
Story, by M. de Montesquieu," Edinburgh (2), I (March-April
1785) [a different translation from the Universal's].

MONTOLIEU, ISABELLE, baronne DE, 1751–1832

*Caroline de Litchfield, ou mémoires extraits des papiers d'une famille
prussienne. Par Madame de *＊*. 2 vols. Londres et Paris, 1786:
*Caroline of Litchfield, a Novel. Translated from the French. By
Thomas Holcroft. 3 vols. London: Robinson, 1786; rptd. Dublin,
1786 [Summers]; 2nd ed., 1787 [Summers]; rptd. Ireland, 1795
[Summers].

ORMOY, CHARLOTTE CHAUMAY D'

*Les Malheurs de la jeune Emélie, pour servir d'instruction aux âmes
vertueuses et sensibles. Paris, 1777: "Amelia, a Novel. From the
French of Madam d'Ormoy," Caledonian Magazine and Review,
I (May 1783)–III (April 1784) [a note on page 148 declares it to
be "a genuine translation and indeed the first that has ever made
its appearance in the English language"].

PREVOST, ANTOINE FRANÇOIS, known as Prévost d'Exiles,
1697–1763

*Le Doyen de Killerine, histoire morale. Paris, 1733: *The Dean of
Coleraine. A moral history: founded on the memoirs of an illus-
trious family in Ireland. A New Edition, Carefully Corrected and
Improved. 2 vols. London: Jullion, 1780 [a reissue of the original
1742-43 translation].
Histoire de Marguerite d'Anjou, reine d'Angleterre. 1740 [Bibliothè-
que Nationale]: *The History of Lady Anne Neville, Sister to the
Great Earl of Warwick; In Which Are interspersed Memoirs of

that Nobleman, and the Principal Characters of the Age in which she lived. 2 vols. London: Cadell, 1776 [Alexander Bicknell, the author, declares in his introduction, "I acknowledge myself greatly indebted to Monsieur L'Abbé Prevôst for many Incidents of my Heroine's life; and have generally followed his Account of them," p. xi; there had been one translation already in 1755].

*Manon Lescaut, Vol. VII of *Mémoires d'un homme de qualité.* Paris, 1731: *The History of the Chevalier des Grieux; written by himself. Translated from the French.* 2 vols. London: White, 1767 [*Monthly;* extracted from the 1743 *Marquis de Bretagne* version; see below]; *Manon L'Escaut; or, the fatal attachment. A French story. Translated by Mrs. Charlotte Smith.* 2 vols. London: Cadell, 1785 [F.M. Hilbish, *Charlotte Smith, poet and novelist (1749–1806).* Philadelphia, 1941].

*Mémoires et avantures d'un homme de qualité qui s'est retiré du monde. 7 vols. Paris, 1728–31: **Memoirs of a man of quality. Written originally in the French Tongue, by Himself, after his Retirement from the World. A new edition.* 2 vols. London: Newbery, 1770 [reissue of an original 1738 translation]; **The Memoirs and Adventures of the Marquis de Bretagne and the Duc d'Harcourt. To which is added, The History of the Chevalier de Grieu and Moll Lescaut, an extravagant Love-adventure. Translated from the Original French, By Mr. Erskine.* 3 vols. London: Cooper, 1770 [reissue of an original 1743 translation].

*Le Philosophe anglais, ou histoire de M. Cleveland, fils naturel de Cromwell, écrite par lui-même. 8 vols. Paris, 1731–39: **The Life and Entertaining Adventures of Mr. Cleveland, Natural Son of Oliver Cromwell, Written by Himself. The Third Edition, Corrected.* 4 vols. London: Rivington, Fletcher, etc., 1760 [the first edition appeared in 1734–35]; *Cleveland.* 1780 [Block].

RICCOBONI, MARIE JEANNE, 1713–1792

"L'Aveugle" [original appearance unidentified]: **"The Blindman, a Fairy-Tale, translated from the French of Madam Riccoboni," Universal,* XXXVII (August 1765).

——: *The Continuation of the life of Mariane. To which is added, The History of Ernestina, with Letters and other Miscellaneous Pieces.* London: Becket, 1766 [publisher's advertisement; exact French original unidentified, but perhaps this is a translation of *Recueil de pièces détachées.* Paris, 1765].

*Histoire d'Adelaide de Dammartin, comtesse de Sancerre. 2 vols.

Paris, 1766; retitled in 1767 *Lettres d'Adelaide de Dammartin, comtesse de Sancerre, à M. le comte de Nancé, son ami, par Madame Riccoboni:* *Letters from the Countess de Sancerre, to Count de Nancé, her friend. By Madam Riccoboni. Translated from the French.* 2 vols. London: Becket and De Hondt, 1767.

**Histoire de Christine, reine de Suabe; et celle d'Aloïse de Livarot. Par Madame Riccoboni.* Paris, 1783: *The History of Christina, princess of Swabia; and of Eloisa de Livarot. Translated from the French of Madame Riccoboni.* London: Stockdale, 1784 [Library of Congress].

Histoire de Miss Jenny, écrite et envoyée par elle à Milady C* de Roscomond. Par Mme Riccoboni.* 4 vols. Paris, 1764: **The History of Miss Jenny Salisbury; addressed to the Countess of Roscommond. Translated from the French of the celebrated Madame Riccoboni.* 2 vols. London: Becket and De Hondt, 1764; "History of Miss Jenny, Written and Sent by Her to the Countess of Roscommon, Lady to the English Ambassador at the Court of Denmark. Translated from the French of Madame Riccoboni," *Universal,* XXXV (September-December 1764).

L'Histoire de M. le Marquis de Cressy, traduite de l'anglois par Mme de *.* Amsterdam, 1758: **The History of the Marquis de Cressy. Translated from the French.* London: Becket and De Hondt, 1765 [first issued in 1759]; *"Memoirs of Madame Riccoboni. Extracted from Mrs. Thicknesse's *Sketches of the Lives and Writings of the Ladies of France,*" *Lady's,* XIII (December 1782)–XIV (February 1783).

**Lettres de Elisabeth-Sophie de Vallière à Louise Hortense de Canteleu, son amie, par Mme Riccoboni.* 2 vols. Paris, 1772: **Letters from Elizabeth Sophia de Valiere to her Friend Louisa Hortensia de Canteleu. By Madam Riccoboni. Translated from the French by Mr. Maceuen.* 2 vols. London: Becket, 1772.

**Lettres de Milady Juliette Catesby à Milady Henriette Campley, son amie.* Amsterdam, 1759: **Letters from Juliet Lady Catesby, To her Friend Lady Henrietta Campley. Translated from the French* [by Frances Brooke]. London: Dodsley, 1760; 4th ed., 1764 [British Museum]; rptd. 1769 [NCBEL]; 6th ed., 1780 [British Museum].

**Lettres de Mistriss Fanni Butlerd à milord Charles Alfred de Caitombridge, comte de Plisinth, duc de Raflingth. Ecrites en 1735. Traduites de l'anglais en 1755 par Adelaide de Varançai.* Paris, 1757: *Letters of Fanny Butler.* 2 vols. London: Becket, ca. 1766 [cited in the publisher's list at the end of *The History of the Marquis de Cressy*, hence the vague date; I have, however, found no other record of publication].

Lettres de mylord Rivers à Sir Charles Cardigan, entremêlées d'une partie de ses correspondances à Londres pendant son séjour en France, par Mme Riccoboni. 2 vols. Paris, 1776: *Letters from Lord Rivers to Sir Charles Cardigan, and to other English correspondents, While he resided in France. Translated from the original French of Madame Riccoboni, by Percival Stockdale.* 2 vols. London: Becket, 1778.

——: *Select novels, containing The Blindboy, a fairy tale; Indian letters, and The distressed orphan, or adventures of Ernestina. Translated from the French of Mme Riccoboni.* London: Lane, 1781.

Les Vrais Caractères du sentiment, ou Histoire d'Ernestine. Liège, 1765; later titled simply *Histoire d'Ernestine.* Paris, 1766: *"The History of Ernestine, Translated from the French of Mme Riccoboni," Universal,* XXXVII (September-October 1765) [first English translation]; also "The History of Ernestine," *Weekly Amusement,* IV (December 1767); likewise *Weekly Miscellany* (Glasgow), n.s. II, Nos. 31–37 (February-March 1793) [for other appearances of this story between hard covers, see RICCOBONI, *Continuation of the Life of Mariane* and *Select novels*].

RICHER, ADRIEN, 1720–1798

Essai sur les grands événements par les petites causes, tiré de l'histoire. Genève et Paris, 1758 [Bibliothèque Nationale]: *Great Events from Little Causes. Or, a selection of Interesting and Entertaining Stories, Drawn from the Histories of different Nations. Wherein Certain Circumstances, seemingly inconsiderable, are discovered to have been apparently productive of very Extraordinary Incidents. Translated from the French of Monsieur A. Richer, by whom it was dedicated by Permission, to her most serene Highness the late Duchess of Orleans.* London: Newbery, 1767 [Block].

ROUSSEAU, JEAN-JACQUES, 1712–1778

——: *The Beauties of Rousseau, selected by a Lady* [Eliza Roberts]. 2 vols. London: Hookham, 1788 [*Monthly*].

Julie ou la nouvelle Héloïse. Lettres de deux amants habitants d'une petite ville au pied des Alpes, recueillies et publiées par Jean-Jacques Rousseau. 6 vols. Amsterdam, 1761: *Eloisa, or a Series of*

Original Letters. Collected and Published by J.J. Rousseau. Translated from the French [by William Kenrick]. 4 vols. London: Griffiths, and Becket and De Hondt, 1761; rptd. Dublin: Hunter, 1761; 2nd ed. London, 1761; 3rd ed., 1764; *Julia; or the New Eloisa* (Vols. I–III of *Works*). Edinburgh, 1773; *Eloisa; or a series of Original Letters.* 4 vols. 1776; *Eloisa, a new Edition; to which is now first added, the sequel of Julia, or the New Eloisa.* 1784 [the sequel is *Laura*; see below]; rptd. Edinburgh, 1794; *Eloisa, a new Edition, to which are Added, the Adventures of Lord B—— at Rome, being the Sequel of Eloisa.* 2 vols. 1795; rptd. Dublin, 1795; *"The History of Juliet, or the Modern Eloisa," London,* XXX (March, April, July, September, October 1761) [original translation of various letters]; also *"Two Letters from Eloisa," Universal,* XXIX (August-September 1761); also *Review, with considerable quotation, Critical,* XIII (September 1761); also *Plot summary and quotation, Monthly,* XXV (September-October 1761).

—— [French original nonexistent]: *Laura; or, Original letters. In two volumes. A sequel to the Eloisa of J.J. Rousseau. From the French.* London: Lane, 1790 [a spurious attribution; actually from F. A. C. Werthes, *Begebenheiten Eduard Bomstons in Italien,* via a French translation entitled *Les Amours de Milord Edouard Bomston;* Blakey].

—— [French original nonexistent]: *Letters of an Italian Nun and an English Gentleman. Translated from the French of J.J. Rousseau.* London: Bew, 1781 [a spurious attribution, according to Th. Dufour's bibliography of the works of Rousseau]; 2nd ed., 1781 [Bibliothèque Nationale]; rptd. 1784 [NCBEL].

RUTLEDGE, JEAN-JACQUES, 1742–1794

Mémoires de Julie de M . . . 1790 [Monglond]: *Memoirs of Julia de M***, a reclaimed Courtesan. From the French of Le Chevalier Rutledge, Author of La Quinzaine Anglaise.* 2 vols. London: Bentley, 1791 [misprinted 1741; Summers].

SAINT-LAMBERT, JEAN FRANÇOIS, marquis DE, 1716–1803

"Sara Th. . .., Nouvelle traduite de l'Anglois," Gazette littéraire de l'Europe, 17 août 1765: *"Sara Th——; or, the Discovery, a Novel," Universal,* XLV (October 1769); also "The Story of Sarah Phillips, a Novel, by M. de Saint Lambert," *Lady's,* XXIII (September-October 1792) [taken from *Tales, Romances, etc.;* see ANTHOLOGIES].

SAINT-PIERRE, JACQUES HENRI BERNARDIN DE, 1737–1814

*La Chaumière indienne. Paris, 1791: *The Indian Cottage. Translated from the French of Monsieur de St. Pierre, author of Etudes de la Nature, Paul et Virginie, etc. [by E. A. Kendall]. London: Bew, 1791; The Indian Cottage; or, A Search after truth. From the French of M. Saint Pierre [translated by E. A. Kendall]. London: Lane, 1791 [Blakey]; rptd. Workington: Richardson, 1797 [British Museum]; rptd. London: Lane, 1799 [British Museum]; *The Indian Cottage. By James Henry Bernardin de Saint Pierre. Translated by E. A. Kendal. London: Vernor and Hood, 1800; "The Indian Cottage, a Tale. Translated from the French for the Bee," Bee, XVII (September-October 1793).

*Paul et Virginie [Vol. IV of Etudes de la Nature]. Paris, 1788: Paul and Virginie. With a frontispiece, an engraved title, and four plates by G. Barrett. London, 1788 [Block]; *Paul and Mary, an Indian Story. 2 vols. London: Dodsley, 1789 [translated by Daniel Malthus]; rptd. Dublin, 1789 [NCBEL]; The Shipwreck; or, Paul and Mary. London: Lane, 1790 [Block]; *Paul and Virginia. Translated from the French of Bernardin de Saint-Pierre; by Helen Maria Williams. [no imprint] 1795; *rptd. London: Robinson, 1795; *rptd. London: Vernor and Hood, 1796; rptd., n.d. [New York Public Library]; Studies of Nature. By James-Henry-Bernardin de Saint Pierre. Tr. by Henry Hunter. London: Dilly, 1796 [Vol. V is Paul and Virginia; Library of Congress]; *"The Children of the Cottages," in Beauties of Saint-Pierre: selected from his Studies of Nature. By Edward Augustus Kendall. London: Vernor and Hood, 1797; rptd. 1799 [New York Public Library]; "The History of Paul and Virginia, Translated from the French of Bernardin St. Pierre, by Miss Helen Maria Williams," Weekly Entertainer, XXIX (February-May 1797).

SENAC DE MEILHAN, GABRIEL, 1736–1803

*Les Deux Cousins, histoire véritable. Paris, 1790: *The Cousins of Schiras. Translated from the French by John Brereton Birch, Esq. 2 vols. London: Lane, 1797.

SOUSA BOTELHO MOURAO E VASCONCELLOS, ADELAIDE, comtesse Flahaut, marqueza DO, known as Mme de Souza, 1761?–1836

*Emilie et Alphonse, ou danger de se livrer à ses premières impressions. Par l'auteur d'Adèle de Senange. 2 vols. Paris, An VII [1799]:

Emilia and Alphonsus, a Novel, translated from the French. 2 vols. 1799 [Block].

TENCIN, CLAUDINE ALEXANDRINE GUERIN DE, 1681–1749

*Mémoires du Comte de Comminge. Paris, 1735: **Memoirs of the Count Comminges; or, the Unhappy Lovers. Translated from the French. With a Sketch of the Abbey of La Trappe in Normandy, the Members of which are enjoined to perpetual Silence. By Monsieur D'Arnaud, of the Royal Academy of Berlin, and Counsellor to the French Embassy at Dresden.* London: Kearsley, 1774 [falsely attributed to D'Arnaud, probably because all French editions of his play *Le Comte de Comminge* were preceded by Mme de Tencin's story, which he had simply adapted dramatically]; "The History of the Count de Comminge, Written by Himself," *Lady's Museum,* I, Nos. 2–8 (1760) [translated by Charlotte Lennox]; also "Memoirs of the Count d'Comminge, and Adelaid, of Laussan. Translated from the French of Monsieur D'Arnaud," *Universal,* LVI (February-March 1775) [an abridgement of Kearsley's publication]; likewise *Edinburgh Magazine and Review,* V (February 1776); also "The History of the Count de Comminge, Written by Himself," *Town and Country,* XIII (January-Supplement 1781); likewise *Hibernian Magazine* (February 1781-January 1782); also "The History of the Count de Comminge, Supposed to be Written by Himself. Translated from the French, by Mrs. Lennox," *New Novelist's,* II (1787).

THIBOUVILLE, HENRI LAMBERT D'ERBIGNY, *marquis* DE

*Le Danger des passions, ou anecdotes syriennes et égyptiennes. Traduction nouvelle. Par l'auteur de L'Ecole de l'amitié. 2 vols. [no imprint] 1751: *The Danger of the Passions; or, Syrian and Egyptian Anecdotes. Translated from the French of the Author of The School of Friendship.* 2 vols. London: Evans, 1770 [*Gentleman's*].

USSIEUX, LOUIS D', 1744–1805

*Clemence d'Entragues, ou le siège d'Aubigny, anecdote française. Par M. d'Ussieux. Paris, 1773: *The Siege of Aubigny. An Historical Novel. By Major Mante.* London: Hookham, 1781 [Summers].

AN INDEX TO THE ENGLISH TITLES OF TRANSLATED FRENCH SENTIMENTAL FICTION

1. "Abbas and Sohry": see BRICAIRE DE LA DIXMERIE, "Abbas et Sohry"
2. "Account of Numa Pompilius": see FLORIAN, *Numa Pompilius*
3. "Account of the Letters of the Marquis de Roselle": see ELIE DE BEAUMONT, *Lettres du Marquis de Roselle*
4. "Adela and Theodore": see GENLIS, *Adèle et Théodore*
5. *Adelaide and Theodore* [novel and magazine appearances]: see GENLIS, *Adèle et Théodore*
6. *Adelaide; or, Conjugal Affection*: see MASSON DE MORVILLIERS, *Adelaide*
7. "The Adventures of Alphonso and Marina": see FLORIAN, "Célestine"
8. *The Adventures of Numa Pompilius*: see FLORIAN, *Numa Pompilius*
9. "The Adventures of the Baron de Lovzinski": see LOUVET DE COUVRAI, *Une Année de la vie du Chevalier de Faublas*
10. "Affecting History of St. Andre": see GENLIS, "Histoire de St. André"
11. *The Age of Chivalry*: see GENLIS, *Les Chevaliers du cygne*
12. *Aglaura. A Tale*: see MARMONTEL, "La Bergère des Alpes"
13. "Albertina": see BONNEVILLE, "Albertine"
14. "Alexis, or the Cottage in the Woods": see DUCRAY-DUMINIL, *Alexis*
15. "All or Nothing": see MARMONTEL, "Tout ou rien"
16. "Amelia, a Novel": see ORMOY, *Les Malheurs de la jeune Emélie*
17. *An Amorous Tale of the Chaste Loves of Peter the Long*: see BILLARDON DE SAUVIGNY, *Histoire amoureuse de Pierre Le Long*
18. "Anette and Lubin"—"Annete and Lubin": see MARMONTEL, "Annette et Lubin"
19. "Arsaces and Ismena": see MONTESQUIEU, "Arsace et Isménie"
20. *Aspasia; or, The Dangers of Vanity*: see BENOIT, *Les Aveux d'une jolie femme*
21. "Azakia": see BRICAIRE DE LA DIXMERIE, "Azakia"

22. "The Bad Mother": see MARMONTEL, "La Mauvaise Mère"
23. "Bathmendi": see FLORIAN, "Bathmendi," and ANTHOLOGIES, *Tales, Romances, etc.*
24. *The Beauties of Genlis*: see GENLIS
25. *The Beauties of Rousseau*: see ROUSSEAU
26. *Belisarius* [novel and magazine appearances]: see MARMONTEL, *Bélisaire*
27. "Benevolence and Gratitude": see ARNAUD, "Sidney et Volsan"
28. *Blansay*: see GORJY, *Blançay*
29. "The Blindman": see RICCOBONI, "L'Aveugle," and *Select novels*

30. "Camira": see FLORIAN, "Camiré"
31. *Caroline of Litchfield*: see MONTOLIEU, *Caroline de Litchfield*
32. "The Casket": see MARMONTEL, "La Cassette"
33. *Cecilia: or the Eastern Lovers*: see CARRA, *Odazir*
34. "The Character of Richardson": see ARNAUD, "La Nouvelle Clémentine"
35. "The Characters of Prévôt, Le Sage, Richardson, Fielding, and Rousseau": see ANONYMOUS
36. *Charite and Polydorus*: see BARTHELEMY, *Les Amours de Carite et Polydore*
37. *The Child of Nature, Improved by Chance* [novel and magazine appearances]: see HELVETIUS
38. "The Children of the Cottages": see SAINT-PIERRE, *Paul et Virginie*
39. "Claudina"—"Claudine": see FLORIAN, "Claudine"
40. "Cleomar and Dalia"—"Cleomir and Dalia": see BRICAIRE DE LA DIXMERIE, "Cléomir et Dalia"
41. *Cleveland*: see PREVOST, *Le Philosophe anglais*
42. *Confessions of a Beauty*: see ANONYMOUS
43. "The Connoisseur": see MARMONTEL, "Le Connoisseur"
44. "The Constant Lovers": see FLORIAN, "Célestine," and ANTHOLOGIES, *Tales, Romances, etc.*
45. *The Continuation of the life of Mariane*: see RICCOBONI
46. *The Correspondence of Two Lovers*: See LEONARD, *Lettres de deux amans*
47. *The Count de Rathel*: see ANONYMOUS, *The Count de Rethel*
48. *The Count de Rethel*: see ANONYMOUS
49. *A Course of Gallantries*: see DUCLOS, *Les Confessions du comte de* ***

76. "The Favourite": see MARMONTEL, "La Mauvaise Mère"
77. "Female Fortitude": see GENLIS, "Histoire de la Duchesse de C***"
78. *The Foresters*: see ANONYMOUS
79. *The Friend of Virtue*: see FONTANIEU
80. "Friendship put to the Test": see MARMONTEL, "L'Amitié à l'épreuve"

81. *Galatea*: see FLORIAN, *Galatée*, and *Oeuvres*
82. "The Generous Lady": see ANONYMOUS, "La Dame généreuse"
83. "Giaffar and Abassah": see BRICAIRE DE LA DIXMERIE, "Giaffar et Abassah"
84. *Gonsalva of Cordova—Gonzalva of Cordova—*"Gonzalo de Cordova": see FLORIAN, *Gonzalve de Cordoue*
85. "The Good Mother": see MARMONTEL, "La Bonne Mère"
86. "The Good Sovereign": see CUBIERES, *Misogug*
87. "The Good Wife": see MARMONTEL, "La Femme comme il y en a peu"
88. *Great Events from Little Causes*: see RICHER, *Essai sur les grands événements*

89. "Happily": see MARMONTEL, "Heureusement"
90. "The Happy Divorce": see MARMONTEL, "L'Heureux Divorce"
91. "The Happy Repentance": see ARNAUD, *Fanni*
92. "Heroick Virtue": see ANONYMOUS
93. "Histoire de la ruine de la ville de Mexico": see MARMONTEL, *Les Incas*
94. "The History of Alsaleh": see ANONYMOUS, and ANTHOLOGIES, *Pictures of the Heart*
95. "History of Celestia": see LE PRINCE DE BEAUMONT, "Histoire de Céleste"
96. *The History of Christina, princess of Swabia*: see RICCOBONI, *Histoire de Christine*
97. *The History of Count Gleichen*: see ARNAUD, "Le Comte de Gleichen"
98. "The History of Ernestine": see RICCOBONI, *Les Vrais Caractères du sentiment, Continuation of the life of Mariane*, and *Select novels*
99. "History of Francis Count Montgomery and the Sieur d'Anglade": see ANONYMOUS
100. "The History of James Le Brun": see GAYOT DE PITAVAL, *Causes célèbres et intéressantes*

126. *Joseph. A Poem*: see BITAUBE, *Joseph*
127. *Julia; or the New Eloisa*: see ROUSSEAU, *Julie*
128. "Julia, or the Penitent Daughter": see ARNAUD, "Julie"
129. *Julius; or, The Natural Son*: see LOAISEL DE TREOGATE, *Le Fils naturel*

130. *The Knights of the Swan*: see GENLIS, *Les Chevaliers du cygne*

131. *Laura, or Letters from Switzerland*: see CONSTANT DE REBECQUE, *Laure*
132. *Laura; or, Original Letters*: see ROUSSEAU
133. "Lauretta": see MARMONTEL, "Laurette"
134. "Lausus and Lydia": see MARMONTEL, "Lausus et Lydie"
135. *Leonora*: see ANONYMOUS
136. "A Lesson from Adversity": see MARMONTEL, "La Leçon du malheur"
137. "The Lesson of Misfortune": see MARMONTEL, "La Leçon du malheur"
138. "Letter from a Peruvian Princess to her Lover": see GRAFFIGNY, *Lettres d'une Péruvienne*
139. *Letters from Elizabeth Sophia de Valiere*: see RICCOBONI, *Lettres de Elisabeth-Sophie de Vallière*
140. *Letters from Emerance to Lucy*: see LE PRINCE DE BEAUMONT, *Lettres d'Emerance à Lucie*
141. *Letters from Juliet Lady Catesby*: see RICCOBONI, *Lettres de Milady Juliette Catesby*
142. *Letters from Lord Rivers*: see RICCOBONI, *Lettres de mylord Rivers*
143. *Letters from the Countess de Sancerre*: see RICCOBONI, *Histoire d'Adelaide de Dammartin*
144. "Letters of a Peruvian Princess": see GRAFFIGNY, *Lettres d'une Péruvienne*
145. *Letters of an Italian Nun*: see ROUSSEAU
146. "Letters of Aza": see LAMARCHE-COURMONT, *Lettres d'Aza*, and GRAFFIGNY, *Lettres d'une Péruvienne*
147. *Letters of Fanny Butler*: see RICCOBONI, *Lettres de Mistriss Fanni Butlerd*
148. *Letters of Madame du Montier*: see LE PRINCE DE BEAUMONT, *Lettres de Madame du Montier*
149. *Letters written by a Peruvian Princess*: see GRAFFIGNY, *Lettres d'une Péruvienne*

179. *Moral Tales*: see LE PRINCE DE BEAUMONT, *Contes moraux*
180. *Moral Tales*: see MARMONTEL, *Contes moraux*
181. "The Mutual Astonishment": see BRICAIRE DE LA DIXMERIE, "L'Etonnement réciproque"
182. *Mutual Attachment*: see BASTIDE, *Les Aventures de Victoire Ponty*
183. "The Mutual Surprize": see BRICAIRE DE LA DIXMERIE, "L'Etonnement réciproque"

184. *The Natural Son*: see LOAISEL DE TREOGATE, *Le Fils naturel*
185. *The Negro as there are few white men*: see LAVALLEE, *Le Nègre, comme il y a peu de blancs*
186. *The Negro, Equalled by Few Europeans* [novel and magazine appearances]: see LAVALLEE, *Le Nègre, comme il y a peu de blancs*
187. *The New Clarissa*: see LE PRINCE DE BEAUMONT, *La Nouvelle Clarice*
188. "The New Clementina": see ARNAUD, "La Nouvelle Clémentine"
189. *A New Collection of Moral Tales*: see MARMONTEL, *Nouveaux Contes moraux*
190. *New Moral Tales*: see MARMONTEL, *Nouveaux Contes moraux*
191. *New Tales*: see FLORIAN, *Nouvelles nouvelles*
192. "Le Nourisson": see ANONYMOUS

193. "The Officious Friend": see BEAURIEU, *L'Elève de la Nature*
194. "Olympia, or the Acquisitions of Experience": see LE PRINCE DE BEAUMONT, "Le Juge de sa propre faute"
195. "Optimism, a Dream": see MERCIER, "L'Optimisme"
196. "The Oracle": see BRICAIRE DE LA DIXMERIE, "L'Oracle journalier"
197. "Osman, or Modern Gratitude": see ANONYMOUS

198. *The Palace of Silence*: see ARCQ, *Le Palais du silence*
199. *Paul and Mary, an Indian Story*: see SAINT-PIERRE, *Paul et Virginie*
200. *Paul and Virginia*: see SAINT-PIERRE, *Paul et Virginie*
201. *Paul and Virginie*: see SAINT-PIERRE, *Paul et Virginie*
202. *Pauline; or, The Victim of the Heart*: see CONTANT D'ORVILLE
203. "The Penitent Daughter": see ANONYMOUS
204. *The Peruvian Letters*: see GRAFFIGNY, *Lettres d'une Péruvienne*
205. *The Philosophy of Pleasure*: see HELVETIUS
206. *Pieces from M. de Florian*: see FLORIAN

207. *The Pleasures of Retirement*: see DUCLOS, *Les Confessions du comte de* ***
208. "The Pretended Martin Guerre": see GAYOT DE PITAVAL, *Causes célèbres et intéressantes*
209. "The Pretended Philosopher": see MARMONTEL, "Le Philosophe soi-disant"
210. "The Prince of Brittany": see ARNAUD, "Le Prince de Bretagne"
211. "The Pyrenean Hermits": see BRICAIRE DE LA DIXMERIE, "Les Solitaires des Pyrénées"

212. *Rash Vows*: see GENLIS, *Les Voeux téméraires*
213. "Raymond and Clementina": see ARNAUD, "D'Almanzi"
214. "The Recluses of Murcia": see MARMONTEL, "Les Solitaires de Murcie"
215. *The Rival Mothers*: see GENLIS, *Les Mères rivales*
216. "The Rival Princes": see ANONYMOUS
217. *The Romance of Real Life*: see GAYOT DE PITAVAL, *Causes célèbres et intéressantes*
218. "Rosetta, a Tale": see IMBERT, "Rosette"
219. "Rural Probity": see ANONYMOUS

220. *St. Alma*: see GORJY, *Saint Alme*
221. "Sara Th——; or, the Discovery": see SAINT-LAMBERT, "Sara Th..."
222. "The School for Fathers": see MARMONTEL, "L'Ecole des pères"
223. *Select Moral Tales*: see MARMONTEL, *Contes moraux*
224. *Select novels*: see RICCOBONI
225. "The Self-Rival": see ANONYMOUS
226. "Selico": see FLORIAN, "Selico," and *Nouvelles nouvelles*
227. "The Sentimental Coquette": see ANONYMOUS
228. *Sentimental Tablets of the Good Pamphile*: see GORJY, *Tablettes sentimentales du bon Pamphile*
229. "The Sequel of the Peruvian Princess": see LAMARCHE-COURMONT, *Lettres d'Aza*
230. "Seraphina, a Novel": see MERCIER, "Vivonne et Ruyter"
231. *The Shepherdess of the Alps* [novel and magazine appearances]: see MARMONTEL, "La Bergère des Alpes"
232. *Sheridan and Kotzebue*: see MARMONTEL, *Les Incas*
233. *The Shipwreck and Adventures of Mons. Pierre Viaud* [novel and magazine appearances]: see DUBOIS-FONTANELLE, *Naufrage et aventures de M. Pierre Viaud*

234. *The Shipwreck; or, Paul and Mary*: see SAINT-PIERRE, *Paul et Virginie*
235. *The Siege of Aubigny*: see USSIEUX, *Clemence d'Entragues*
236. "The Slave of Sensuality": see GENLIS, "Histoire de M. de la Palinière"
237. "Soliman the Second"—"Solyman the Second": see MARMONTEL, "Soliman II"
238. "Sophronius": see FLORIAN, "Sophronime"
239. *Stella. A pastoral romance*: see FLORIAN, *Estelle*
240. "The Story of Sarah Phillips": see SAINT-LAMBERT, "Sara Th...," and ANTHOLOGIES, *Tales, Romances, etc.*
241. *Studies of Nature*: see SAINT-PIERRE, *Paul et Virginie*
242. *Suzette's Dowry*: see FIEVEE, *La Dot de Suzette*
243. "The Sylph": see ANONYMOUS
244. "The Sylph Husband": see MARMONTEL, "Le Mari sylphe"

245. *The Tales of an Evening*: see MARMONTEL, *Nouveaux Contes moraux*
246. *Tales of the Castle*: see GENLIS, *Les Veillées du château*
247. *Tales. Translated from the French of M. Marmontel*: see MARMONTEL, *Nouveaux Contes moraux*
248. *The Tears of Sensibility*: see ARNAUD, *Les Epreuves du sentiment*
249. *The Temple of Gnidus, and Arsaces and Ismenia*: see MONTESQUIEU, "Arsace et Isménie"
250. "There Was no Help for it": see MARMONTEL, "Il le fallait"
251. *The Transmigrations of Hermes* [novel and magazine appearances]: see FAUQUES, *Les Transmigrations d'Hermès*
252. "The Travels of Heraclitus and Democritus": see BRICAIRE DE LA DIXMERIE, "Héraclite et Démocrite, voyageurs"
253. "The Trial of Friendship": see MARMONTEL, "L'Amitié à l'épreuve"
254. *The Triumph of Truth*: see LE PRINCE DE BEAUMONT, *Le Triomphe de la vérité*
255. *The True and Surprising Adventures ... of Mons. Pierre Viaud*: see DUBOIS-FONTANELLE, *Naufrage et aventures de M. Pierre Viaud*
256. "The True Point of Honour": see LE PRINCE DE BEAUMONT, "Le Vrai Point d'honneur"
257. "Two Letters from Eloisa": see ROUSSEAU, *Julie*
258. "The Two Unfortunate Ladies": see MARMONTEL, "Les Deux Infortunées"

INDEX